The Kaizen Way

Embracing Small Changes for Big Impact

Michael Yoshida

Table of Contents

INTRODUCTION

The Japanese concept of Kaizen, which promotes the value of gradual, tiny advancements, is a light of wisdom in a world where people are fixated on instant results and success. Kaizen is the result of combining the Japanese terms "kai" (change) and "zen" (good). It means "change for the better" or "continuous improvement." Some of the most prosperous companies in the world have adopted this methodology, but its ideas can also be reasonably practical in our own lives.

It is not necessary to make significant adjustments or drastic overhauls in order to achieve personal and professional greatness. Instead, it necessitates a dedication to gradually implementing tiny, doable adjustments over time. The goal of this book, "The Kaizen Way: Embracing Small Changes for Big Impact," is to walk you through the ideas and methods of Kaizen and show you how this way of thinking may change your life little by little.

Japanese culture has strong roots in kaizen, especially during the post-World War II period when Japan was reconstructing its economy. American business techniques served as an inspiration for Japanese inventors, who improved upon them to create Kaizen, which is now a vital element of Japan's industrial success. Businesses such as Toyota used Kaizen to improve their manufacturing processes, which resulted in the creation of the Toyota Production System, which is a globally recognized model of effectiveness and quality.

Fundamentally, Kaizen is a way of thinking rather than merely a collection of methods or instruments. It involves creating an environment in which all members of a community or organization are welcome to offer ideas and proposals for advancement. Instead of drastic change, the emphasis is on group improvement made little by little. This way of thinking is easily applied to personal growth and provides a long-term, sustainable route to reaching objectives.

Within the context of personal growth, Kaizen motivates us to pinpoint our areas of weakness and implement gradual, manageable adjustments. The secret is to start small, whether it's with developing new talents, relationships, or healthy habits. Over time, these little adjustments can have a compounding impact that results in significant alteration.

Think about your regular activities and routines. Are there any small changes you may make to enhance your health and happiness? Maybe it's taking a five-minute meditation break every morning, fitting in a quick stroll, or cutting back on sugar gradually. Even though these little things might not seem like much on their own, when they are regularly performed, they gain momentum and provide noticeable gains.

In the workplace, the Kaizen idea is also quite successful. Employees at all levels are enabled to contribute to the success of the firm by emphasizing continual development. This promotes a healthy work atmosphere where creativity and innovation can flourish, in addition to increasing productivity and efficiency.

Putting Kaizen into practice at work entails developing a culture that values the opinions of all team members. Easy procedures like conducting frequent feedback meetings, recognizing minor achievements, and promoting experimentation can have a significant impact on an organization's performance as a whole. The tenets of Kaizen support the development of productive teams, enhance leadership, and promote long-term growth.

This book is filled with motivational tales of people and businesses who have adopted Kaizen and seen remarkable outcomes. These case studies demonstrate the transformative potential of tiny changes by providing real-world experiences. These tales demonstrate how Kaizen can be applied anywhere, from business success stories to personal accounts of increased health and wellbeing.

Your manual for embracing a Kaizen mentality is "The Kaizen Way: Embracing Small Changes for Big Impact." It will provide you with the resources and know-how to bring about ongoing development in all facets of your life. By the time you finish reading this book, you will know that modest, conscious steps made repeatedly over time add up to long-lasting success and fulfillment rather than sudden, large-scale changes.

Set out on this adventure with an open mind and a readiness to take little steps forward. In addition to assisting you in reaching your objectives, the Kaizen route promises to foster a lifetime appreciation for the wonders of continuous improvement.

CHAPTER I

The Origins of Kaizen

The Birth of Kaizen in Japan

The Japanese phrase "change for the better" (kaizen) refers to a philosophy that has had a significant influence on the contemporary world, particularly in the areas of business and personal growth. It is necessary to examine the historical, cultural, and economic factors that influenced the development of Kaizen in Japan in order to comprehend its origins. The history of Kaizen is closely related to the post-World War II recovery of Japan, the impact of American management techniques, and the distinctive features of Japanese culture.

Following World War II, Japan was faced with the enormous challenge of reconstructing its infrastructure and economy. The nation was in ruins, its economy in tatters, and its industries devastated. But the Japanese people started an incredible journey of rebuilding, motivated by a strong work ethic and a deep-seated desire to restore their nation's prosperity and dignity. The rebuilding phase created an ideal environment for the growth of Kaizen.

American statistician and management consultant Dr. W. Edwards Deming was a pivotal contributor to the early development of Kaizen. Early in the 1950s, Japan recruited Deming to assist in enhancing its ind ustrial procedures. He brought statistical quality control and the significance of continual improvement to Japanese management. Deming's theories placed a strong emphasis on the idea that quality should not just be ensured by inspection at the end of the production line but should be integrated into the process from the start. His concepts struck a deep chord with Japanese managers and served as the impetus for the development of the Kaizen philosophy.

Joseph M. Juran, an expert in quality management from the United States, was another key figure in the development of Kaizen. Similar to Deming, Juran received an invitation to Japan to impart his knowledge of quality control. He presented the idea of "quality circles," which were small groups of employees that got together on a regular basis to talk about and resolve issues pertaining to their work procedures. This cooperative method of problem-solving became a cornerstone of Kaizen, encouraging staff engagement and a continuous improvement culture.

It is impossible to exaggerate Deming and Juran's impact on Japanese management techniques. It is important to note, nevertheless, that Japanese culture was not wholly unfamiliar with the ideas they brought. In actuality, a lot of the principles and practices of Kaizen are very similar to those of traditional Japan. In Japan, collaboration, respect for others, and an emphasis on the process rather than the outcome are highly valued. These cultural elements were a significant contributing factor in the quick uptake and incorporation of Kaizen concepts in Japanese companies.

The Toyota Production System is among the most prominent instances of Kaizen in action (TPS). In the 1950s, as Toyota found it challenging to compete with Western automakers, it implemented Kaizen concepts to transform its manufacturing procedures. Toyota established a system that prioritized waste reduction, respect for employees, and continual improvement under the direction of Taiichi Ohno and Eiji Toyoda. The TPS rose to prominence as an example of effectiveness and caliber, establishing new benchmarks for the global automotive sector.

At Toyota, the concept of Kaizen was introduced through a number of crucial procedures that are now widely associated with it. Among these is "just-in-time" production, which tries to cut inventory costs by manufacturing only what is required, when required. This strategy guarantees resource efficiency and reduces waste. At Toyota, a crucial component of Kaizen is the implementation of "jidoka," or "automation with a human touch." This idea entails building systems and procedures so that they can automatically identify and address issues, freeing up employees to concentrate on ongoing development and problem-solving.

The concept of "gemba," which translates to "the real place" in Japanese, is a fundamental component of Kaizen. The term "Gemba" in Kaizen refers to the location of value creation, which is usually the factory floor or the service delivery location. The Gemba principle highlights how crucial it is to identify the problem's root cause in order to properly comprehend it and create workable solutions. By using a hands-on approach, improvements are guaranteed to be grounded in real situations and data, not conjecture or hearsay.

The Kaizen philosophy also stresses how important it is for leaders to cultivate a culture of ongoing improvement. Leaders in Kaizen-practicing firms are required to set an example for the attitudes and behaviors they value in their staff members. This entails a dedication to education, an openness to hearing criticism and offering constructive criticism, and an emphasis on human development. Through fostering an atmosphere that values and encourages ongoing development, leaders may motivate their people to take responsibility for their work and pursue greatness.

Numerous important reasons have contributed to Kaizen's success in Japan. First off, teamwork and collaboration are fundamental to Japanese management and work practices. The adoption of quality circles and gemba walks by Japanese companies was facilitated by this cultural inclination. Second, the post-war era's social and economic strains engendered a sense of urgency and a readiness to accept novel concepts. In order to compete in the world market, Japanese businesses were driven to enhance their operations and output, and Kaizen offered a valuable and efficient framework for doing so.

In addition, the incorporation of Kaizen ideas into Japanese training and education programs contributed to their broad acceptance and long-term viability. To ensure that the legacy of Kaizen is continued, educational institutions have included lectures on quality management and continuous improvement in their curricula. The focus on training and education has contributed to the deep integration of Kaizen throughout Japanese industry and society.

The ideas of Kaizen have become popular outside of Japan throughout time, impacting corporate strategy and management techniques all across the world. Kaizen has been used by businesses across a range of sectors, including technology, healthcare, and manufacturing, to improve operations and spur innovation. Kaizen's global reach attests to its adaptability and efficacy as a continuous improvement concept.

In summary, the history of Kaizen in Japan is one of resiliency, cooperation, and cross-cultural understanding. Japan adopted and assimilated the continuous improvement concepts pioneered by Juran and Deming, together with traditional Japanese values, after emerging from the ruins of World War II. The ability of little, gradual adjustments to produce significant, long-lasting gains was shown by the success of Kaizen at organizations like Toyota. Today, Kaizen still serves as a source of inspiration for people and organizations all over the world to pursue improvement relentlessly in order to achieve greatness. The legacy of Kaizen serves as a constant reminder that, despite the difficulties we encounter, we can always do better and that even the slightest adjustments can have a significant influence.

Key Figures and Influencers

Influential individuals and influencers have had a significant impact on human history, culture, and society via their deeds, thoughts, and leadership. These people have made a lasting impact on the globe; they include social reformers, political figures, scientists, and artists. This section examines the lives and accomplishments of some of the most significant people in a variety of fields, emphasizing the enduring legacy they have left behind.

Mahatma Gandhi is among the most important political figures in contemporary history. In addition to helping India gain independence from British rule, his nonviolent and civil disobedient mindset served as an inspiration for civil rights organizations around the world. Gandhi's conviction that nonviolent resistance may bring about social and political transformation served as the foundation for his dedication to nonviolence. Millions were inspired by his leadership during the Indian independence movement, which proved the power of group action based on moral values. Gandhi's impact went beyond India; in the United States, leaders like Martin Luther King Jr. were influenced by Gandhi and used nonviolent tactics to fight for civil rights.

Another legendary character in political history is Winston Churchill, who is best remembered for his command during World War II. In his capacity as British Prime Minister, Churchill's unwavering determination and stirring speeches played a pivotal role in galvanizing the British populace amidst the most dire moments of the conflict. His perseverance and eloquence bolstered the spirit of the country and encouraged resiliency and resolve. Churchill left behind a complicated legacy that is shaped by both his leadership during the war and his influence on the post-war world, but there is no denying his historical significance and the significant impact a determined leader can have during difficult times.

Few people have had as much of an impact on social reform as Nelson Mandela. His fight against South Africa's apartheid system and his eventual election as the nation's first black president serve as an example of the resilience and forgiving nature needed to triumph against structural injustice. Despite serving 27 years in prison, Mandela's dedication to nation-building and reconciliation served as a model for addressing entrenched social divides around the world. His leadership during South Africa's transition from apartheid to democracy left a lasting legacy for his country and as a representation of the global struggle for justice and equality.

In the field of science, Albert Einstein is regarded as one of the most significant individuals of the 20th century. His theory of relativity transformed our perception of gravity, space, and time and established the foundation for a large portion of contemporary physics. Beyond his contributions to theoretical physics, Einstein was a fervent supporter of world peace and a strong opponent of nuclear weapons. His achievements in science and his dedication to humanitarian causes have elevated him to the status of an enduring symbol of moral rectitude and intellectual success.

Artists like William Shakespeare and Leonardo da Vinci have had a profound impact on human culture. Leonardo da Vinci is the Renaissance's poster child for the polymath, thanks to his achievements as an inventor, scientist, and painter. His scientific research and inventions demonstrate a mind well ahead of its time, and his masterpieces, including The Last Supper and the Mona Lisa, never cease to enthrall audiences. The fusion of science and art by Leonardo da Vinci is a prime example of the inventiveness and curiosity of people.

Shakespeare, who is sometimes called the best writer in the English language, has had a significant impact on both theater and literature. His plays, which have found an audience across generations and nations, explore universal themes of human nature, power, and fate. Notable examples of these themes are Hamlet, Othello, and Macbeth. Shakespeare's literary skills and profound comprehension of human nature have made his works timeless and highly esteemed, resulting in constant adaptations and reinterpretations for upcoming generations.

Modern art has been greatly influenced by artists and cultural icons, such as Pablo Picasso, who transformed visual arts. Picasso paved the way for the rise of Cubism, which upended preconceived notions and created new forms of artistic expression. He became a pivotal character in 20th-century art due to his incessant capacity to innovate and reinvent himself. He influenced a significant number of artists and shaped the course of modern art movements.

People like Leo Tolstoy and Jane Austen have had a lasting impact on literature. Jane Austen provided sharp commentary on gender roles, social class, and romantic relationships in early 19th-century England in her books Pride and Prejudice and Sense and Sensibility. Her books are enduringly famous and influential in both literary and popular culture thanks to her astute observations and biting wit. Comparably, against the backdrop of Russian society, Leo Tolstoy's epic works, such as War and Peace and Anna Karenina, examine the intricacies of human experience. Tolstoy is regarded as one of the finest authors in global literature because of his broad narrative style and deep insights into human nature.

Composers like Ludwig van Beethoven and contemporary music superstars like The Beatles have had a significant cultural influence. Beethoven's works, especially his piano pieces and symphonies, revolutionized musical structure and emotional expression. Being able to use music to communicate profound human experiences has elevated him to a prominent position in the Western classical tradition. Conversely, The Beatles' avant-garde songwriting and recording methods transformed popular music during the 1900s. Their impact went beyond music to include fashion, movies, and social movements, making them historical and cultural icons.

The field of philosophy and thought is another area where significant individuals have an impact. The intellectual underpinnings of cultures have been altered by individuals like Karl Marx, Confucius, and Socrates. Western philosophy was founded on the questioning and dialogue techniques of Socrates, which emphasized the value of introspection and critical thought. His theories continue to be a mainstay of philosophical education and have influenced other thinkers.

Chinese culture and ethics have been significantly impacted by Confucius, whose teachings serve as the foundation of Confucianism. For millennia, the values and social structures of East Asian countries have been influenced by his emphasis on morality, social harmony, and filial devotion. Confucian philosophy still has a significant impact on current Asian debates about ethics and government.

The Communist Manifesto and Das Kapital, in particular, written by Karl Marx, have had a significant influence on political theory and practice. Marx's analysis of capitalism and his idea of a society without classes served as an inspiration for revolutionary movements and the creation of socialist nations during the twentieth century. Even though his theories have been used and understood in a variety of ways, Marxist theory continues to have a significant impact on the political and economic debate of today.

People like Marie Curie and Isaac Newton have produced revolutionary advances in science and technology. In addition to laying the groundwork for classical mechanics, Isaac Newton's theories of motion and universal gravitation had a significant impact on the scientific revolution. His contributions to mathematics, especially the creation of calculus, have had a long-lasting effect on a number of scientific fields.

Marie Curie received two Nobel Prizes for her groundbreaking studies on radioactivity, which also cleared new paths in chemistry and physics. Her discoveries benefited industry and medicine in addition to furthering scientific understanding. Curie is a role model for future generations of scientists, especially women in

STEM professions, because of her commitment to science and her ground-breaking accomplishments.

People like Malala Yousafzai and Martin Luther King Jr. have had a significant influence on social justice and human rights. The American civil rights movement was greatly aided by Martin Luther King Jr.'s leadership, especially in promoting peaceful protest as a means of opposing racial injustice and segregation. His moving writings and speeches, including the well-known "I Have a Dream" address, continue to motivate movements for equality and justice all around the world.

The youngest Nobel laureate, Malala Yousafzai, is now well-known throughout the world for supporting women's rights and girls' education. Malala has used her platform to speak out against tyranny and to advocate for educational opportunities for girls globally since escaping a Taliban attempt on her life. Her bravery and advocacy work have raised awareness of gender equality and the value of education on a global scale.

Influential personalities also have an impact on innovation and entrepreneurship; Steve Jobs, for example, revolutionized business and technology. Steve Jobs was a co-founder of Apple Inc., and his vision and leadership propelled the creation of ground-breaking devices, including the iPad, MacBook, and iPhone. His emphasis on innovation, design, and user experience revolutionized the technology sector and changed how people use technology on a daily basis.

Sports celebrities like Serena Williams and Muhammad Ali have not only had remarkable success, but they have also utilized their platforms to speak out about social issues. In addition to being recognized as one of the all-time great boxers, Muhammad Ali was well-known for his vocal support of civil rights and opposition to the Vietnam War. He became a symbol of resistance and resiliency because of his bravery in sticking up for his convictions despite the tremendous personal cost.

One of the greatest tennis players of all time, Serena Williams, has defied prejudices in the sports industry and broken several records. Her domination on the tennis court, along with her support of racial and gender equality, has elevated her to the status of an influential figure in the sports industry and beyond.

In summary, influential people from a variety of fields have had a significant impact on how human history and society have developed. Whether in politics, science, the arts, social justice, or other sectors, their efforts have created enduring legacies that inspire and influence people all around the world. These people's lives and accomplishments show the value of advocacy, leadership, and creativity in bringing about social and cultural change. They also illustrate the long-lasting impact of those who have the courage to question the status quo and dream of a better future for humanity.

Kaizen vs. Western Improvement Strategies

Kaizen, a Japanese concept that translates to "continuous improvement," and Western improvement tactics are two different ways that organizations can increase production, quality, and efficiency. Both approaches seek to promote change, but they are very different in terms of their guiding ideas, workings, and cultural foundations. This section explores the fundamental concepts of both Kaizen and Western improvement strategies, contrasting their methods, uses, advantages, and drawbacks to offer a thorough grasp of how both strategies affect organizational development.

Deeply ingrained in Japanese culture and management philosophy, kaizen stresses small, ongoing changes that involve all staff members, from front-line staff to upper management. Its foundation is the notion that gradual, constructive adjustments over time can result in notable advancements. After Toyota incorporated the Kaizen concept into the Toyota Production System (TPS), it gained international recognition and helped the business establish a reputation for quality and efficiency in manufacturing.

The idea that every employee has intrinsic worth and potential is one of the core principles of Kaizen. This kind of thinking promotes a culture in which workers are constantly seeking methods to streamline their workflows and cut down on waste. Kaizen is distinguished by its emphasis on tiny, controllable adjustments as opposed to significant overhauls. These modifications are frequently carried out through cooperative efforts at what is referred to as "Kaizen events" or "Kaizen blitzes," where cross-functional teams gather to quickly discover issues, suggest fixes, and test those fixes.

The fully participatory nature of kaizen's approach to development depends on the skills and imagination of workers at all levels. Because employees are actively involved in the process of finding and implementing improvements, this inclusivity develops a sense of ownership and accountability among them. Furthermore, standardization and the methodical removal of waste, or "muda," which includes tasks that do not improve the good or service, are highly valued aspects of Kaizen.

In contrast, top-down initiatives driven by data analysis and expert-led projects are typically the emphasis of Western improvement techniques, which are commonly associated with methodologies like Six Sigma, Lean, and Total Quality Management (TQM). Although these tactics also seek to improve productivity and quality, they frequently depend on specific expertise and equipment to recognize and resolve problems. Six Sigma, for instance, emphasizes a rigorous, data-driven approach to problem-solving and applies statistical methods to eliminate variation and flaws in processes. Lean, which originated in the TPS but was modified for use in the West, seeks to optimize workflows and remove waste in order to speed processes.

The way that Kaizen and Western improvement methodologies approach change is one of their main distinctions. Western approaches frequently entail more significant, more revolutionary undertakings carried out by expert teams or consultants. Although these initiatives have the potential to produce substantial gains, they could also be more disruptive and resource-intensive. On the other hand, Kaizen is less disruptive and more long-lasting due to its emphasis on minor, ongoing improvements. Kaizen may make a company more robust and adaptive by promoting a culture of minor, frequent enhancements.

The significance of employee involvement and leadership is another noteworthy differentiation. Leadership frequently takes on a more directive role in Western improvement efforts, establishing objectives and guiding initiatives via official programs. Because of this, there may occasionally be a gulf between frontline staff and management because the latter may not feel as empowered or involved in the process of change. Conversely, kaizen encourages a more inclusive and cooperative strategy in which managers support and encourage staff-driven advancements. Employee engagement and sense of ownership may increase as a result, making the team more driven and united.

Western improvement techniques and kaizen techniques each have advantages and disadvantages of their own. Kaizen places a significant emphasis on minor, ongoing improvements that can make an organization more flexible and long-lasting while also fostering a strong sense of employee ownership and commitment. However, this strategy may also take longer to produce noticeable, substantial outcomes, and it necessitates strong support and buy-in from all organizational levels. Furthermore, the capacity to sustain momentum and avoid complacency over time is a critical component of the success of Kaizen projects.

Western improvement tactics can provide more noticeable and significant gains more quickly since they concentrate on expert-led, data-driven projects. These approaches are frequently excellent for handling challenging issues that need specific training and equipment. They can, however, also be more disruptive and resource-intensive, and their success often hinges on their capacity to successfully manage change and guarantee alignment among various organizational levels. Moreover, the hierarchical structure of numerous Western approaches may result in a deficiency of involvement and accountability among frontline staff members, impeding the sustainability of the enterprise over an extended period.

In spite of these distinctions, there is a great deal of room for combining aspects of Western and Kaizen improvement techniques to provide a more well-rounded and successful organizational development strategy. For example, companies might use the specific tools and approaches of Western methodologies like Six Sigma and Lean while simultaneously embracing Kaizen's emphasis on employee involvement and continual development. Organizations can solve their individual limits and capitalize on the advantages of both strategies by integrating them.

Creating a hybrid model that combines the most effective elements of Western and Kaizen methodologies is one way to accomplish this integration. In addition to executing structured, data-driven projects to solve more complicated issues, this model could entail cultivating a culture of continuous improvement and employee involvement. It is the responsibility of leaders to create an atmosphere that is conducive to experimentation, teamwork, and learning from both achievements and setbacks in order to facilitate this integration.

Programs for training and development can also aid in bridging the knowledge gap between Western improvement techniques and Kaizen. Organizations may develop a workforce that is more adaptable and competent by providing workers with the information and abilities required to take part in both incremental and radical improvement projects. In order to do this, training in Kaizen practices and principles, as well as Six Sigma, Lean, and other Western methodologies' tools and techniques, may be provided.

Aligning improvement initiatives with company goals and strategies is another crucial factor to take into account. A thorough grasp of the organization's goals and priorities should serve as the foundation for both Kaizen and Western improvement techniques. This calls for efficient coordination and communication between organizational levels as well as the capacity to monitor and assess the results of improvement initiatives. Organizations may optimize their influence and promote significant, long-lasting transformation by guaranteeing that their improvement endeavors are in line with their overarching objectives.

Organizations can also gain from benchmarking against industry standards and studying best practices from outside sources in addition to these internal initiatives. Businesses can learn a great deal and spot areas for development by examining the achievements and difficulties of other companies that have adopted Kaizen and other Western improvement techniques. This may entail attending industry conferences, interacting with professional networks, and working on improvement projects in conjunction with other organizations.

To sum up, there are two different but complementary methods of organizational improvement: Kaizen and Western improvement strategies. Although Kaizen places a strong focus on employee involvement and ongoing, incremental improvements, Western approaches like Six Sigma and Lean provide solid tools and techniques for tackling complex issues and achieving significant improvements. Organizations can design an improvement plan that is more effective and balanced by taking into account the advantages and disadvantages of both approaches. By incorporating these approaches and dedicating resources to alignment, training, and outside education, businesses can strengthen their capacity to produce long-lasting gains and promote sustained success.

CHAPTER II

The Philosophy of Continuous Improvement

Principles of Kaizen

The Japanese word "kaizen," which means "continuous improvement," is the cornerstone of a management concept that has had a significant impact on business operations all over the world. Kaizen, a Japanese concept, emphasizes the value of gradually improving processes, efficiency, and quality by making tiny, consistent adjustments over time. This strategy emphasizes the importance of teamwork, employee involvement, and a commitment to long-term improvement in contrast to the Western concentration on large-scale, radical reforms. The foundational ideas of Kaizen are examined in this section, along with its applications and effects on performance and corporate culture.

The emphasis on continuous improvement is one of the core tenets of Kaizen. This idea stems from the conviction that there is always space for improvement and that no system or procedure is flawless. Constant process evaluation, problem-solving, and small-scale, doable adjustments are all part of continuous improvement. Organizations can move forward steadily without the disturbance that more significant improvements frequently bring about thanks to this iterative method. Kaizen offers a culture of constant improvement, which motivates workers at all levels to look for and apply improvements in their everyday work.

Another essential component of Kaizen is employee involvement. In contrast to conventional top-down management strategies, Kaizen places a strong emphasis on the active participation of every employee, from senior managers to front-line staff. This inclusive approach is predicated on the understanding that those who carry out the task are frequently in the best position to spot inefficiencies and suggest workable fixes. Employee participation in the improvement process develops a sense of accountability and ownership in addition to utilizing their knowledge and experience. This may result in higher levels of drive, contentment at work, and a more profound dedication to the objectives of the company.

The implementation of Kaizen events, or "blitzes," is a crucial part of employee involvement in Kaizen. Cross-functional teams collaborate on these targeted, brief initiatives to solve specific issues or areas that could be used better. In these sessions, members of the team work together to examine procedures, find the sources of problems, and create and test fixes. Kaizen events are fast and interactive, which enables firms to make changes rapidly and evaluate their effects. This promotes a flexible and adaptable approach to improvement.

Another essential Kaizen element is standardization. In order to get ongoing enhancement, it is vital to implement and preserve uniform procedures. Standardization guarantees that effective changes are implemented uniformly throughout the company and offers a baseline from which progress can be evaluated. This entails putting best practices in writing, establishing precise rules, and updating protocols often to take into account fresh ideas and discoveries. Organizations can lower variability, improve quality, and expedite processes by upholding strict standards and guaranteeing consistency.

Reducing waste, or "muda," is the primary goal of Kaizen. Any effort that does not improve the product or service from the standpoint of the consumer is considered waste. The Kaizen philosophy divides waste into seven categories: flaws, inventory, motion, overproduction, waiting, transportation, and overprocessing. Organizations can decrease expenses, increase customer happiness, and increase efficiency by methodically identifying and getting rid of certain kinds of waste. This emphasis on cutting waste promotes a leaner, more flexible approach to operations, which helps businesses adapt more quickly to shifting consumer demands and market conditions.

A key component of Kaizen is the idea of quality at the source. This idea highlights the significance of dealing with problems at the source as opposed to depending just on inspection and repair. By enabling workers to spot and fix errors in real-time, companies can stop issues from getting worse and guarantee better results. Quality at the source promotes a proactive approach to quality management by giving staff members the resources, instruction, and authority to make corrections. Lowering the need for expensive rework and adjustments not only raises operational efficiency but also improves the quality of the goods and services provided.

Kaizen also highlights how crucial having a long-term outlook is. The strategy is centered on creating tiny, gradual improvements, but it is also informed by a dedication to long-term, sustainable improvement. This idea pushes businesses to think more broadly about how their decisions will affect their performance and success in the long run rather than just focusing on the present. In a corporate environment that is changing quickly, Kaizen helps firms maintain their competitiveness and build resilience by promoting a culture of continuous learning and adaptation.

The ideas of continuous improvement and incremental improvement are closely related. Kaizen promotes minor, incremental improvements over significant, disruptive overhauls. This strategy reduces resistance to change since workers are more likely to accept and adjust to minor changes than to significant ones. Additionally, by allowing businesses to test and fine-tune changes prior to scaling them up, incremental improvements lower the possibility of unexpected repercussions and guarantee that improvements are both long-lasting and successful.

The application of data and metrics to direct improvement initiatives is another fundamental tenet of kaizen. Making decisions based on data is crucial for pinpointing problem areas, tracking advancement, and evaluating the effects of adjustments. Kaizen pushes businesses to gather and examine pertinent data in order to understand the effectiveness of their processes and pinpoint the underlying causes of problems. This evidence-based approach guarantees that improvements are made based on objective analysis rather than conjecture or intuition and that improvement efforts are concentrated on areas with the most significant potential for effect.

The core of the Kaizen concept is the idea of cooperation and teamwork. Cross-functional teams with a variety of backgrounds and specialties usually lead Kaizen improvement projects. By allowing team members to draw from their diverse backgrounds and experiences, this collaborative approach encourages innovation. Additionally, teamwork fosters a sense of responsibility and a common goal, which increases commitment to and involvement with the process of improvement. Employees can accomplish more substantial and long-lasting gains when they collaborate rather than when they work alone.

Additionally, Kaizen emphasizes management support and leadership strongly. Leaders who are dedicated to the ideas of continuous improvement and who actively support and promote improvement initiatives are necessary for the successful implementation of Kaizen. This entails fostering an atmosphere where staff members are encouraged to propose and carry out improvements, giving them the tools and training they need, and acknowledging and applauding their accomplishments. When it comes to Kaizen, effective leadership is defined by a readiness to pay attention to staff members, support experimentation, and cultivate a culture of ongoing learning and development.

Enhancing organizational culture is one of the significant advantages of Kaizen. Through the integration of employee involvement, cooperation, and continuous improvement into the organization's core values, Kaizen cultivates a culture that values excellence and creativity. This change in culture has the potential to boost commitment and loyalty among staff members as well as promote job satisfaction and employee engagement. Businesses that use Kaizen frequently discover that their staff members are more driven and aggressive in looking for and putting improvements into practice, which results in long-term performance increases and a competitive edge.

Kaizen has significant advantages for operations as well. Organizations can significantly increase productivity and efficiency by concentrating on reducing waste, standardizing procedures, and improving quality. Kaizen's stepwise approach guarantees the long-term sustainability of these advantages by gradually integrating changes into routine activities. Because they are constantly monitoring and improving their processes to adjust to changing conditions and client requests, this method also enables firms to be more responsive and agile.

The effect that Kaizen has on customer satisfaction is another significant feature. Kaizen focuses on adding value from the customer's point of view and prioritizes quality from the source, which helps businesses produce higher-quality goods and services. A more substantial reputation and brand image, as well as more customer satisfaction and loyalty, can result from this customer-centric strategy. Businesses that continuously provide high-quality goods and services are in a better position to draw in new clients and keep existing ones, which promotes long-term success and expansion.

While kaizen has numerous advantages, there are drawbacks as well. The necessity for a culture change is one of the main obstacles, especially in companies with long-standing hierarchies and top-down management practices. Making the shift to a Kaizen strategy necessitates a mental shift where all staff members are motivated to actively participate in attempts to improve. Without strong leadership and a resolute dedication to the Kaizen principles, this can be challenging to accomplish.

Preventing complacency and keeping up the momentum are two more challenges. Because Kaizen is incremental in nature, changes are frequently made gradually, and after initial benefits are made, it can be simple for organizations to get complacent. It takes constant work, frequent process evaluations, and a dedication to looking for new opportunities for improvement to sustain a culture of continuous improvement. It is imperative for organizations to exercise vigilance in guaranteeing the constant application of effective adjustments and the frequent updating of standards to incorporate novel insights and innovations.

Development and training are essential for implementing Kaizen successfully. Workers must possess the abilities and information necessary to recognize inefficiencies, make suggestions for improvements, and carry out adjustments. This entails offering instruction in process improvement tools and methodologies as well as Kaizen practices and ideas. Employee engagement and their ability to contribute to the process of change depend on ongoing development and assistance.

To sum up, the tenets of Kaizen provide a strong foundation for attaining ongoing development and boosting organizational effectiveness. Kaizen promotes a culture of excellence, creativity, and cooperation by concentrating on tiny, gradual improvements, including every employee, and placing a strong emphasis on standardization and waste elimination. Kaizen offers numerous advantages, such as enhanced productivity, superior quality, more customer happiness, and a more enthusiastic and involved workforce. Ongoing training and development, firm adherence to the Kaizen principles, and competent leadership are necessary for successful implementation, nevertheless. Organizations may maintain a competitive edge in a constantly evolving business environment and achieve lasting performance gains by adopting these concepts and cultivating a culture of continuous improvement.

Mindset of Incremental Change

The incremental change mindset is a practical and philosophical approach to improvement that stresses making gradual, tiny changes over time in order to have significant, long-term effects. This kind of thinking is essential to many methods and techniques in corporate management and personal development, including Kaizen, Agile, and continuous improvement. Fundamentally, the incremental change approach is about cultivating a culture of perseverance and flexibility, realizing the significance of tiny steps over time, and appreciating their potential. This section examines the fundamentals, advantages, uses, and difficulties of embracing an incremental change attitude, emphasizing the significant effects it has on people and organizations.

The idea that significant improvement comes from many tiny, manageable steps rather than a few vast, drastic enhancements is one of the core tenets of the incremental change philosophy. This idea stems from the knowledge that significant life changes can be intimidating and dangerous, frequently resulting in resistance and failure. More minor adjustments, on the other hand, are more straightforward to execute, easier to manage, and less disruptive. Individuals and organizations can gain momentum, stay motivated, and make sustainable progress over time by concentrating on minor improvements.

The mentality of gradual transformation promotes an emphasis on ongoing learning and adaptation. It acknowledges that development and improvement are constant processes and that there is always room for progress. This kind of thinking encourages people to be curious and receptive to new ideas, and it makes teams and individuals continuously look for methods to improve productivity and results. People who embrace lifelong learning become more resilient and adept at navigating the intricacies and uncertainties of their surroundings.

The emphasis on experimentation and iteration is a crucial component of the gradual change mindset. With this method, little modifications are tested, input is gathered, and changes are made in response to the findings. It is consistent with the scientific method, which bases findings on empirical data and tests ideas through experiments. Through this iterative process, both individuals and organizations can improve their performance over time by improving their techniques and learning from their experiences. The incremental change mindset lessens the fear of making mistakes and promotes a more creative and proactive attitude by appreciating experimentation and learning from mistakes.

The incremental change approach is centered on the idea of patience. It necessitates an awareness that real change takes time and that it's not always possible to get results right away. This long-term view encourages people and organizations to stick with their objectives in the face of obstacles and setbacks. Additionally, perseverance is cultivated by patience, which motivates people to stick with a plan and keep making tiny changes even when things appear to be moving slowly. The incremental change mentality fosters resilience and drive by keeping an eye on the big picture.

Systems thinking is a fundamental component of incremental change. This method entails comprehending the interactions and influences between various system components. Individuals and organizations can find leverage points—places where minor adjustments can have a significant impact—by realizing these interdependencies. A holistic approach to improvement is promoted by systems thinking, in which decisions are made after taking into account their broader effects. This viewpoint guarantees that changes are long-lasting and in line with overarching objectives while also assisting in preventing unforeseen effects.

There are several advantages to the incremental change mindset for both people and businesses. The decrease in aversion to change is one of the most enormous benefits. Large-scale changes frequently need significant revisions and have a larger chance of failing, which makes them scary and likely to encounter resistance. More minor, gradual adjustments, on the other hand, are easier to handle and are less likely to meet with resistance. They enable teams and people to adjust progressively to new working practices, which gradually increases confidence and buy-in.

The potential to achieve ongoing improvement is another advantage. The mindset of incremental change promotes a continuous search for methods to improve results and performance. As a result, there is a culture of constant adaptation and progress, where advancements are found and made. Individuals and organizations can make significant cumulative improvements and stay competitive by continuously making tiny modifications.

A more inventive and proactive culture is also promoted by the incremental change approach. This strategy encourages people and teams to take chances and investigate novel concepts by appreciating experimentation and learning from mistakes. People may become more innovative and creative as a result of feeling more free to try out novel ideas and gain knowledge from their mistakes. An organization that is more resilient and agile is better able to react to opportunities and changing conditions. This is made possible by the emphasis on ongoing learning and adaptation.

The incremental change mentality has the potential to provide significant and long-lasting growth in the area of personal development. Through the establishment of modest, attainable objectives and persistent effort towards them, people can form new routines, acquire new abilities, and realize their dreams. Because the development is observable and achievable, this strategy aids in sustaining momentum and drive. Because the emphasis is on small stages rather than drastic changes, it also lowers the danger of burnout and discouragement.

The incremental change mentality has the potential to improve productivity and performance in organizational settings. Organizations may enhance customer happiness, reduce inefficiencies, and improve quality by consistently refining their processes and systems. By concentrating on minor, doable adjustments, resources can be allocated more efficiently because advancements can be made without requiring significant expenditures or disruptions. This strategy may result in an organization that is more responsive and effective, and that can maintain long-term success.

Adopting a gradual change approach is not without its difficulties, though. Keeping up the pace and avoiding complacency is one of the biggest obstacles. Incremental change's slow, progressive pace can occasionally cause a feeling of stagnation, where people lose motivation to develop because they grow accustomed to the status quo. To overcome this obstacle, it is critical to set specific objectives, monitor development on a regular basis, and recognize little victories. People and organizations can continue to be committed to continuous development by keeping an eye on the bigger picture and appreciating the significance of every little step.

Finding a balance between the need for more substantial, transformative changes and incremental change is another difficulty. Even while the incremental change attitude stresses tiny, doable actions, there are situations in which more significant changes are required to meet external demands or accomplish strategic objectives.

Businesses need to become adept at determining when small changes will suffice and when more significant overhauls are needed. To achieve the intended results, this calls for strategic planning, strong leadership, and the capacity to combine incremental and transformative techniques.

Another essential component of the gradual change mindset's effectiveness is effective communication. Ensuring that all stakeholders comprehend the reasoning for minor adjustments, the anticipated advantages, and their part in the development process is crucial. Effective and regular communication promotes cooperation, decreases resistance, and builds alignment. Additionally, it offers a chance to discuss achievements and lessons discovered, highlighting the benefits of the gradual transition strategy and promoting continued involvement.

Fostering and maintaining an incremental change attitude requires strong leadership. The values of experimentation, learning, and continual development must be modeled by leaders. They must establish a setting that rewards creativity, promotes taking risks, and values the contributions of each and every employee. Leaders can enable their teams to drive significant change and take ownership of the improvement process by giving them the tools, training, and support they need. In order to be an effective leader, one must also celebrate the accomplishments of both individuals and groups, emphasize the value of small steps forward, and keep people motivated.

Developing a mindset of incremental transformation requires training and development. Both individuals and groups must possess the abilities and information necessary to spot areas for growth, carry out adjustments, and assess the results. This entails offering instruction in systems thinking, data analysis, and problem-solving methodologies. Employee engagement and their ability to contribute to the process of continuous improvement are both increased with ongoing development and assistance.

In summary, the incremental change attitude highlights the importance of gradual, tiny changes over time and is a potent, transforming approach to improvement. This way of thinking encourages a culture of perseverance, adaptation, and creativity by emphasizing experimentation, continual learning, patience, and systems thinking. Incremental change has many advantages, such as less resistance to change, ongoing progress, higher levels of innovation, and improved performance. Adopting this mindset does, however, come with specific problems, like keeping up momentum, striking a balance between gradual and radical improvements, and making sure that leadership and communication are effective. Long-term success and sustainable advancement can be attained by people and organizations by tackling these issues and adopting the incremental change philosophy.

Kaizen and the Modern Workplace

The Japanese concept of "continuous improvement," or "kaizen," has had a significant impact on contemporary workplace procedures all around the world. Since its inception in Japan following World War II, Kaizen has come to represent effectiveness, improvement of quality, and employee involvement. Its ideas have been widely embraced by a number of industries, changing corporate settings and service sectors in addition to manufacturing. This section examines the fundamental concepts of Kaizen, how it is applied in the contemporary workplace, its advantages, and the difficulties that businesses encounter while implementing this way of thinking.

The fundamental tenet of kaizen is that gradual, tiny adjustments over time can result in significant gains. This strategy stands in stark contrast to the Western tendency for radical, large-scale changes. Kaizen is the practice of continuously and manageably improving processes and establishing an environment where staff members are encouraged to point out inefficiencies and provide suggestions for enhancements. The foundation of this ideology is the conviction that all members of the organization, regardless of rank, possess insightful knowledge that may advance the business.

The foundation of Kaizen is the idea of employee involvement. This translates to giving workers the freedom to actively participate in process development and problem-solving in the modern workplace. Kaizen-embracing organizations promote a bottom-up strategy that values and implements comments and ideas from frontline employees. In addition to utilizing the workforce's collective intelligence, this inclusive culture encourages employee accountability and ownership. Knowing that their efforts have the potential to make a significant impact makes them feel more motivated and involved.

In actuality, Kaizen is frequently carried out through "blitzes," or concentrated, brief initiatives meant to target specific problems. These gatherings unite cross-functional teams to examine procedures, pinpoint the underlying causes of issues, and create and evaluate fixes. Kaizen events are fast and iterative, enabling firms to quickly adopt changes and assess their effects. This practical approach works very well to promote a culture of ongoing learning and adaptation as well as driving instant benefits.

Kaizen also emphasizes the elimination of waste, or "muda." Any activity that does not provide value from the standpoint of the client is considered waste in this sense.

Overproduction, waiting, transferring, overprocessing, inventory, motion, and defects are the seven categories of waste that Kaizen identifies. Organizations can enhance quality, cut expenses, and streamline operations by methodically tackling these areas. This emphasis on waste removal in the workplace today is essential for staying competitive and adapting to the market's ever-changing expectations.

Another fundamental tenet of Kaizen is standardization. Standardized practices must be established and upheld in order for continuous improvement to be successful. This entails putting best practices in writing, establishing precise rules, and updating protocols often to take into account fresh ideas and discoveries. Organizations may duplicate successful practices across teams and regions by ensuring consistency and reliability through standardization. This idea promotes scalability and helps maintain high standards in the modern workplace, enabling businesses to expand without sacrificing effectiveness or quality.

Kaizen is based on the idea of quality at the source. Instead of depending only on inspection and rework, this philosophy emphasizes addressing problems at their source. By enabling workers to spot and fix errors in real-time, companies can stop issues from getting worse and guarantee better results. Encouraging workers to make corrections by giving them the resources, instruction, and power to do so is known as "quality at the source." By lowering the need for expensive rework and adjustments, this proactive strategy not only increases operational efficiency but also improves the quality of the products and services.

In the modern workplace, one of the most significant advantages of Kaizen is the development of a continuous improvement culture. Through the integration of Kaizen concepts into the organizational structure, businesses cultivate a work environment where employees are continuously seeking methods to improve their jobs. This change in culture results in more engaged workers who are more satisfied with their jobs and who are more dedicated to the organization's objectives. Morale is raised, and turnover is decreased when workers feel their contributions are valued and acknowledged.

Kaizen has significant positive effects on operations as well. Organizations can significantly increase productivity and efficiency by concentrating on reducing waste, standardizing procedures, and improving quality. The long-term sustainability of these improvements is ensured by the incremental nature of Kaizen, which allows changes to be progressively incorporated into routine activities. By using this strategy, businesses can become more responsive and agile, consistently improving their operations to meet the demands of their clients and adjust to shifting market conditions.

Additionally, Kaizen aids businesses in raising customer satisfaction levels. Kaizen helps enterprises to provide higher-quality goods and services by emphasizing quality at the source and concentrating on adding value from the customer's perspective. A more substantial reputation and brand image, as well as more customer satisfaction and loyalty, can result from this customer-centric strategy. Businesses that continuously provide high-quality goods and services are in a better position to draw in new clients and keep existing ones, which promotes long-term success and expansion.

The workplace of today is more and more defined by the quick development of technology and changing demands from clients. The flexibility and agility that Kaizen promotes are beneficial in this situation. Businesses that use Kaizen are better able to handle the complexity and unpredictability of today's business climate. In order to stay ahead of the competition, they may adapt swiftly to new possibilities and problems and keep refining their offerings and procedures.

Despite all of its advantages, putting Kaizen into practice in the contemporary workplace can be difficult. Promoting a culture change is one of the main obstacles, especially in companies with long-standing hierarchies and top-down management practices. Making the shift to a Kaizen strategy necessitates a mental shift where all staff members are motivated to actively participate in attempts to improve. Without strong leadership and a resolute dedication to the Kaizen principles, this can be challenging to accomplish.

Preventing complacency and keeping up the momentum are two more challenges. Because Kaizen is incremental in nature, changes are frequently made gradually, and after initial benefits are made, it can be simple for organizations to get complacent. It takes constant work, frequent process evaluations, and a dedication to looking for new opportunities for improvement to sustain a culture of continuous improvement. It is imperative for organizations to exercise vigilance in guaranteeing the constant application of effective adjustments and the frequent updating of standards to incorporate novel insights and innovations.

Development and training are essential for implementing Kaizen successfully. Workers must possess the abilities and information necessary to recognize inefficiencies, make suggestions for improvements, and carry out adjustments. This entails offering instruction in process improvement tools and methodologies as well as Kaizen practices and ideas. Employee engagement and their ability to contribute to the process of continuous improvement are both increased with ongoing development and assistance.

In the contemporary workplace, Kaizen's success also depends on effective communication. Ensuring that all stakeholders comprehend the reasoning for minor adjustments, the anticipated advantages, and their part in the development process is crucial. Effective and regular communication promotes cooperation, decreases resistance, and builds alignment. Additionally, it offers a chance to discuss accomplishments and lessons discovered, highlighting the importance of the Kaizen methodology and promoting continued involvement.

A Kaizen culture must be fostered and maintained, and leadership is essential. The values of experimentation, learning, and continual development must be modeled by leaders. They must establish a setting that rewards creativity, promotes taking risks, and values the contributions of each and every employee. Leaders can enable their teams to drive significant change and take ownership of the improvement process by giving them the tools, training, and support they need. In order to be an effective leader, one must also celebrate the accomplishments of both individuals and groups, emphasize the value of small steps forward, and keep people motivated.

The modern workplace is not limited to manufacturing and production settings when it comes to implementing Kaizen. Kaizen principles have been effectively implemented by the service, healthcare, education, and government sectors to promote improvements. Kaizen, for instance, has been applied in the healthcare industry to improve care quality, shorten wait times, and streamline patient care procedures. Kaizen has been used in education by colleges and universities to boost student experiences, simplify administrative procedures, and promote a continuous learning and development culture.

The modern workplace's incorporation of technology has further improved Kaizen's implementation. More effective data collecting, analysis, and sharing are made possible by digital tools and platforms, and these processes are essential for spotting areas for improvement and gauging the effects of changes. Additionally, technology can help with cooperation and communication, which makes it simpler for cross-functional teams to work together on Kaizen projects. Further boosting the efficacy of Kaizen, automation and artificial intelligence can assist businesses in streamlining operations and getting rid of waste.

The use of Kaizen gains additional dimension due to the global character of contemporary companies. International corporations can use Kaizen to standardize procedures throughout many sites, guaranteeing uniformity and quality while permitting regional modifications. This global viewpoint also fosters innovation by offering chances for best practices to be shared and cross-cultural learning. These outcomes enhance the Kaizen methodology.

To sum up, Kaizen has become an essential component of today's workplace since it provides a strong foundation for attaining ongoing development and raising organizational effectiveness. Kaizen promotes a culture of excellence, creativity, and cooperation by concentrating on tiny, gradual improvements, including every employee, and placing a strong emphasis on standardization and waste elimination. Kaizen offers numerous advantages, such as enhanced productivity, superior quality, more customer happiness, and a more enthusiastic and involved workforce. Ongoing training and development, firm adherence to the Kaizen principles, and competent leadership are necessary for successful implementation, nevertheless. Organizations may maintain a competitive edge in a constantly evolving business environment and achieve lasting performance gains by adopting these concepts and cultivating a culture of continuous improvement. The Kaizen approach fits very well with the fast-paced technical improvements and changing demands of customers in the modern workplace, making it a valuable tactic for businesses aiming for sustained success and expansion.

43

CHAPTER III

Small Steps to Personal Transformation

Identifying Areas for Improvement

Any business looking to gain a competitive edge and long-term success must first identify areas for improvement. This procedure entails methodically assessing the results, methods, and practices of the present to identify inefficiencies, bottlenecks, and areas for improvement. It is a fundamental stage in approaches for continuous improvement, including Kaizen, Six Sigma, and Lean. Organizations may create significant change, optimize resources, and more effectively concentrate their efforts by focusing on identifying areas for improvement. This section examines the significance of pinpointing places in need of development, the approaches taken, the difficulties faced, and the outcomes obtained.

The idea of continuous improvement, which emphasizes constant attempts to develop processes, goods, and services, is fundamental to identifying areas for improvement. This idea is based on the conviction that there is always space for improvement and that no process is flawless. Organizations may remain flexible, adjust to shifting market conditions, and satisfy changing customer expectations by consistently identifying and addressing areas for improvement.

Gaining a comprehensive grasp of the current situation is the first step toward pinpointing areas that require change. This includes sketching out procedures, collecting data on performance measures, and carefully documenting current processes. To visualize processes and spot inefficiencies, methods like flowcharting, value stream mapping, and process mapping are frequently employed. For example, process mapping offers a thorough illustration of the phases in a process, emphasizing duplications, hold-ups, and pointless processes. By distinguishing between operations that add value and those that do not, value stream mapping goes one step further and assists organizations in concentrating their improvement efforts where they will have the most significant impact.

To determine where improvements are needed, data collection and analysis are essential. In order to assess present performance and spot trends and patterns, organizations need to compile pertinent data on key performance indicators (KPIs). Metrics pertaining to effectiveness, efficiency, customer happiness, and financial performance may be included in this data. Organizations can utilize tools like statistical analysis, Pareto analysis, and root cause analysis to make sense of the data and identify specific areas that require attention. Pareto analysis assists in prioritizing issues according to their frequency and impact, whereas statistical analysis enables firms to find deviations and outliers in performance data. On the other hand, root cause analysis goes beyond identifying the fundamental causes of difficulties, making sure that fixes deal with the problems at their core rather than just their symptoms.

Finding areas for development requires the active participation of employees. Workers who are closely involved in daily operations frequently have insightful knowledge about problems and inefficiencies. Surveys, suggestion boxes, and focus groups can be used to engage employees and reveal issues that management might not be aware of. Incorporating staff members into the process of improvement also cultivates a culture of accountability and ownership, which encourages them to actively participate in the success of the company.

Observation and interaction with employees at their workstations, such as via Gemba walks, are techniques that can offer personal insights into operational difficulties and areas for improvement.

Another vital source of information for pinpointing areas that need development is customer feedback. Gaps in product performance, customer satisfaction, and service quality can be found through the experiences and perceptions of customers. Organizations can gain a better understanding of the needs and expectations of their customers by gathering feedback via surveys, interviews, and social media monitoring. Recurring problems and areas that need improvement can also be identified by examining client complaints and service logs. Organizations may make sure that their efforts are in line with consumer expectations and strengthen their competitive position by integrating client input into the improvement process.

Benchmarking is an effective method for pinpointing areas that require improvement. It entails contrasting the performance, procedures, and practices of a company with those of top companies or industry norms. Benchmarking facilitates the identification of adoptable or adaptable best practices and performance gaps. There are several varieties of benchmarking, such as functional benchmarking, which involves comparing with businesses in other industries that excel in particular areas; competitive benchmarking, which consists in comparing with direct competitors; and internal benchmarking, which consists in comparing within the organization. Organizations can uncover novel techniques and create realistic performance targets by studying the best in the field.

The Lean methodology relies heavily on the concept of "muda," or waste, to pinpoint areas that require improvement. Overproduction, waiting, transferring, overprocessing, inventory, motion, and defects are the seven categories of waste that Lean identifies. Organizations can increase quality, save costs, and streamline operations by methodically locating and getting rid of these wastes. Organizational and efficient workspaces can be created with the aid of tools like the 5S method (Sort, Set in order, Shine, Standardize, Sustain), while inventory management and production flow can be optimized with the use of Kanban systems and Just-in-Time (JIT) production techniques.

Another methodology that places a strong emphasis on finding and getting rid of errors and unpredictability in processes is called Six Sigma. Six Sigma programs methodically identify areas for improvement, measure current performance, analyze data to reveal fundamental causes, implement improvements, and develop controls to preserve the benefits. They do this by using the DMAIC framework (Define, Measure, Analyze, Improve, Control). Robust analytical frameworks are provided by Six Sigma techniques including control charts, process capability analysis, and design of experiments for identifying and resolving performance issues.

The Kaizen philosophy is centered on ongoing, small-scale improvements that are motivated by staff involvement. All staff members are encouraged by Kaizen to consistently recommend minor enhancements to their work procedures. By utilizing the workforce's combined knowledge and experience, this bottom-up strategy promotes a continuous development culture. "Blitzes," also known as kaizen events, are concentrated, short-term initiatives that unite cross-functional teams to tackle specific problems. These gatherings speed up problem-solving and improvement implementation, highlighting the effectiveness of teamwork in bringing about change.

Even with the wide range of approaches and resources at their disposal, businesses frequently struggle to pinpoint areas that need improvement. Opposition to change is a significant obstacle. Managers and staff may be hesitant to embrace new procedures or admit inefficiencies because they are afraid of the unknown or worry about taking on more work. Effective communication, education, and participation from all stakeholders in the development process are necessary to overcome opposition. In order to initiate change, show a commitment to ongoing progress, and provide the required resources and support, leadership is essential.

The quality and availability of data present another difficulty. Finding opportunities for development requires accurate and pertinent data, but gathering, storing, and analyzing data can be complex for businesses. Addressing this challenge requires putting in place robust data management systems and guaranteeing data integrity. In order to properly evaluate data and draw actionable insights, firms must also build their analytical capabilities. This can be done by acquiring experts or by training current workers.

It might be challenging to strike a balance between short-term and long-term improvement initiatives. Businesses could be tempted to prioritize short-term successes over longer-term, more complicated problems that call for consistent work. Establishing clear priorities, coordinating improvement initiatives with strategic objectives, and keeping an eye on both gradual and revolutionary changes are all necessary for striking the correct balance. Improvement projects can be kept on track and provide significant outcomes with the support of regular progress reviews and effective project management.

Finding areas for development also necessitates a comprehensive viewpoint. Organizations have to take into account how processes are related to one another and how changes may affect various system components. Finding and resolving core causes rather than just treating symptoms requires systems thinking, which entails comprehending the relationships and interactions within a system. Organizations can prevent unforeseen repercussions and make sure that changes are long-lasting and in line with overall goals by adopting a holistic strategy.

There are several advantages to successfully identifying areas that require development. Enhanced effectiveness and output are some of the most direct advantages. Organizations can attain more excellent production with the same or fewer inputs by improving resource use, cutting waste, and streamlining procedures. Cost reductions, more profitability, and a more formidable competitive position result from this.

Another essential advantage is improved quality. Organizations may enhance customer happiness and loyalty by delivering superior products and services by detecting and resolving flaws and variations. Enhancements in quality also lower warranty, rework, and return costs, which boosts profitability even more.

Finding opportunities for development also promotes an innovative and ongoing learning culture. By motivating staff members to actively look for and recommend changes, companies can access a plethora of creative ideas and problem-solving abilities. This innovative culture propels continuous improvements, maintains the organization's agility, and aids in its ability to adjust to shifting market situations.

A focus on continual development also has a favorable effect on employee morale and engagement. Employees are more likely to feel inspired and engaged when they know that their ideas are valued and that they can help make significant changes. A more consistent and effective workforce is a result of this sense of ownership and involvement, which also lowers turnover and improves job satisfaction.

To sum up, pinpointing opportunities for enhancement is an essential step that supports the effectiveness of continuous improvement approaches like Kaizen, Lean, and Six Sigma. Through methodical assessment of existing procedures, collection and examination of data, engagement of staff and clients, and utilization of benchmarking and best practices, establishments can detect inadequacies and prospects for improvement. The advantages of successfully identifying areas for improvement are significant despite obstacles like reluctance to change, data quality, and striking a balance between short- and long-term efforts. Enhanced quality, increased productivity, innovation, and staff involvement are just a few of the numerous benefits that propel company success and competitive edge. The ability to recognize and address opportunities for improvement will continue to be a critical factor in determining an organization's long-term performance and growth as it navigates the intricacies of the contemporary corporate environment.

Daily Habits and Routines

Our lives are powerfully shaped by our daily routines and habits, which have an impact on our general well-being, productivity, and quality of life. These routines serve as the cornerstone of our lives, directing our approach to goals, time management, and health maintenance. Anyone looking to enhance their personal or professional life must comprehend the significance of daily routines and habits, how they develop, and the effects they have on different facets of our lives. This section explores the importance of routines and everyday habits, the science of habit development, the advantages of creating pleasant routines, and doable methods for creating and sustaining them.

One cannot stress the importance of everyday routines and habits. They provide our life structure and a sense of control and regularity. In the fast-paced world of today, when there are often changes and uncertainties, this structure is extremely crucial because it can reduce tension and anxiety. By creating a routine, we build a solid foundation that makes it easier for us to deal with the difficulties we face every day. By automating actions, routines lessen the mental strain involved in decision-making and free up cognitive resources for more challenging activities. One of the main reasons successful people frequently stress the value of maintaining dependable daily routines is because of this automation.

Understanding how habits are formed and sustained is possible thanks to research on habit formation. The trigger, the routine, and the reward are the three elements of the habit loop, which is the mechanism by which habits are created, according to the study. The routine is the behavior itself, the reward is the positive reinforcement that follows the behavior, and the cue initiates the behavior. The behavior becomes automatic as this loop gets embedded in the brain over time. It's essential to comprehend this process if you want to break bad habits and form new ones. Through the identification and manipulation of cues and rewards linked to a particular behavior, people can effectively mold their habits.

Productivity is one of the main advantages of creating healthy daily routines and behaviors. Routineized duties need less conscious thought and effort, freeing up people's energies for more significant and imaginative pursuits. An exercise regimen, a balanced meal, and job preparation in the morning, for instance, can create a great mood that lasts the entire day and increases efficiency and production. Similar to this, routines like designating particular times for checking emails or working intently can reduce outside distractions and improve attention.

Daily routines and habits can have a significant impact on health and well-being. A healthy lifestyle must include regular exercise, a well-balanced diet, enough sleep, and stress management techniques. Long-term health benefits are promoted when these activities are incorporated into a daily routine and become a consistent part of an individual's life. For example, making it a routine to go to bed and wake up at the same time every day might enhance general wellbeing and the quality of sleep. In a similar vein, a regimen that incorporates regular exercise can improve resilience to stress, emotional well-being, and physical fitness.

Daily routines and behaviors can also have a significant impact on mental health. A sense of consistency and predictability that routines offer can be reassuring and help to lower anxiety. Practicing mindfulness meditation, keeping a journal, or going outside can all help reduce stress and enhance mental health. When these routines are incorporated into daily life, they become effective instruments for preserving mental well-being. Routines involving social contacts and hobbies can also offer emotional support and a sense of fulfillment, which enhances mental health in general.

Daily routines and habits have an impact on one's personal development as well. Regular practices that promote self-improvement include reading, picking up new skills, and making time for introspection and goal-setting. People can fulfill their long-term ambitions by setting aside time each day for activities that promote personal development. A daily reading regimen or online courses, for instance, can increase knowledge and skills and improve professional and personal growth. In a similar vein, making goal-setting and evaluation a regular part of one's daily routine helps maintain motivation and attention.

Effective daily routines and habits need deliberate work and dedication to establish. Setting clear, attainable objectives and identifying the areas of life that need change is the first step. As trying to alter too much at once might result in overwhelm and failure, it is crucial to start simple and work your way up to more complicated habits. For example, a person who wants to get fitter might begin by going for a daily walk of 10 minutes and work their way up to more prolonged and more intense activities.

To create habits, one must be consistent. The habit loop is strengthened by repetition, which gradually makes the behavior more automatic. Adding new habits to routines that already work is also beneficial; this tactic is called habit stacking. For instance, you may incorporate a new habit of performing a few minutes of stretching exercises right after brushing your teeth in the morning. As a result, the two activities become strongly associated, which facilitates the formation of the new habit.

Support and accountability can also increase the chances of forming new behaviors that stick. Motivating and encouraging activities include using a habit-tracking app, joining a club with like interests, and discussing goals with friends or family. Accountability partners can boost the likelihood that new habits will be maintained over time by providing encouragement, acknowledging accomplishments, and guiding through obstacles.

It's critical to understand that obstacles are an inevitable aspect of creating new routines and habits. Rather than becoming demoralized by sporadic failures, people ought to see setbacks as chances to grow and modify their strategy. It can be insightful to consider what led up to the lapse and how it might be avoided going forward. Remaining optimistic and practicing self-compassion is essential for conquering obstacles and remaining dedicated to the intended adjustments.

The environment has a crucial influence on the establishment of habits. The social and physical surroundings can help or impede the formation of new habits. Making the atmosphere conducive to positive habits can simplify and enhance the process. Productive and healthful habits can be facilitated by, for instance, having wholesome snacks on hand, designating a workstation for concentrated work, and reducing outside distractions. Surrounding oneself with encouraging and like-minded people can also serve as motivation and reinforcement for excellent activities.

Daily routines and habits can have a significant impact on professional achievement on the job. A productive work routine requires prioritizing activities, managing time well, and striking a work-life balance. Developing a routine that includes goal-setting, task planning, and frequent breaks can increase output and stave off burnout. Additionally, practices that promote career advancement and job satisfaction include ongoing learning, professional development, and regular communication with coworkers.

The increasing prevalence of work-from-home arrangements brings with it both opportunities and unique obstacles for creating efficient routines. To be productive and preserve well-being in a remote work environment, it's critical to establish boundaries, keep a regular exercise, and make a clear division between work and personal life. A disciplined and well-balanced work-from-home experience can be fostered by instituting routines like starting the workday at the same time, taking planned breaks, and wrapping up at a particular time.

To sum up, daily routines and habits are essential to attaining wellbeing, health, and success in both personal and professional spheres. They offer structure, boost output, promote mental and physical health, and encourage personal development. Numerous facets of life can be significantly improved by comprehending the science of habit development and putting ideas into practice to create and sustain positive routines. People can form habits and routines that encourage long-term success and fulfillment by being deliberate, starting small, being consistent, and utilizing support and the surroundings. The need to develop efficient daily routines and habits grows as life's speed increases. These provide a way to overcome obstacles, accomplish objectives, and live a healthy and fulfilling life.

Overcoming Resistance to Change

Life and organizations will always include change due to societal standards, economic developments, and technological advancements. Resistance to change is a typical phenomenon in both individual and organizational contexts despite the fact that it is inevitable and frequently necessary. Resolving this opposition is essential to launching new projects successfully and preserving a competitive advantage in the marketplace. This section explores the root causes of resistance to change, countermeasures, and the crucial role that leadership plays in enabling smooth transitions.

There are a number of reasons why people resist change, such as routine disruption, fear of the unknown, loss of control, and inclement weather. Since uncertainty about the future generally accompanies change, fear of the unknown may be the primary cause. This worry can show itself as tension and anxiety, which makes people oppose new ideas and adhere to tried-and-true routines. Another critical component is loss of control since change can make people feel helpless in their jobs and surroundings. Employees may view any change as a challenge to their competence and autonomy if they are used to doing things a specific way. In addition, poor timing may make resistance worse. Employee resistance is higher when changes are implemented at times of high stress or when other significant initiatives are in progress. This is because they may feel overburdened. Finally, resistance can also result from disruptions to routines. Individuals form routines and habits that are efficient and comfortable for them, and any change to them may encounter resistance.

Recognizing and addressing these root issues is crucial to successfully overcoming resistance to change. A highly efficacious tactic is communication. Having open, honest, and regular communication helps greatly lessen fear and uncertainty. Employees are less likely to be anxious and resistant to change when leaders clearly explain the rationale behind the change, its advantages, and the implementation strategy. Involving staff members in the process of change can also increase their sense of ownership and control. Employee buy-in and support for the change's execution are higher when they participate in the planning and decision-making process.

Overcoming reluctance to change also requires assistance and training. Employee competence can rise, and fear can be decreased by giving them the abilities and information they need to successfully negotiate the new environment. Workshops, training courses, and ongoing assistance can boost employees' self-esteem and sense of competence, which will increase their openness to change. It's also critical to acknowledge and deal with the emotional effects of change. It is imperative for leaders to recognize the emotions and apprehensions of their staff members, offering comfort and assistance during the shift. This may entail offering stress management courses, counseling services, and fostering an open workplace where staff members feel free to voice any worries.

Overcoming resistance to change can also be significantly aided by incentives and rewards. Employee adoption of change efforts is increased when they are associated with favorable results and incentives. Rewards in money, recognition, promotions, or chances to advance professionally can all be used as incentives. These incentives may encourage staff members to participate in the change process and see it as an opportunity rather than a danger.

The ability to lead is essential for getting over opposition to change. Good leaders create a future that their team members can believe in, inspiring and motivating them along the way. They serve as role models by displaying actions that are consistent with the new course and demonstrating a commitment to the change. Additionally, in order to promote an atmosphere of transparency and trust, leaders should be personable and approachable. Leaders who cultivate a good rapport with their staff are more equipped to handle issues and offer the assistance needed to bring about change.

In particular, transformational leadership works very well to get over people's aversion to change. Transformational leaders cultivate an atmosphere of creativity and innovation by inspiring and motivating their people with a compelling vision. They foster a culture of continuous improvement by encouraging their teams to view change as an opportunity for growth and development. Additionally, these leaders offer customized support, acknowledging and attending to each worker's particular needs and issues. Transformational leaders can lead practical change projects and drastically reduce opposition by fostering a feeling of shared purpose and coordinating the change initiatives with the organization's values and objectives.

Establishing a culture that is flexible and resistant to shifts is also crucial for sustained achievement. Businesses that promote a culture of ongoing learning and development are better able to adapt to change. This entails motivating staff members to try out novel concepts, pick up new abilities, and learn from mistakes. Organizations can foster a culture where change is perceived as a chance for personal development rather than a danger by encouraging a growth mindset.

Another essential element in overcoming opposition to change is employee engagement. Employees who are engaged are more likely to be dedicated to the mission and core values of the company, which makes them more open to initiatives for change. Providing chances for professional advancement and development, acknowledging and rewarding accomplishments, and fostering a happy work environment are all essential components of building employee engagement. Employees are more inclined to support and participate in change projects when they feel appreciated and a part of the company.

Planning and implementation must be done in an organized manner in order to achieve effective change management. This entails establishing precise goals, creating a thorough plan, and keeping track of advancement. Change management frameworks offer organized methods for bringing about change and dealing with resistance. Examples of these are Kotter's 8-Step Change Model and Lewin's Change Management Model. These models stress that in order to guarantee the sustainability of the change, it is critical to instill a feeling of urgency, assemble a coalition of supporters, and reinforce the change.

Overcoming reluctance to change frequently starts with instilling a feeling of urgency. This entails explaining why the change is required and what might happen if nothing is done. Leaders can encourage staff participation in the change process by stressing the dangers of continuing as is and the advantages of the suggested change. Identifying and utilizing important organizational influencers who can promote the change and mobilize others to support it is the first step in forming a coalition of support. These influencers have the power to bring about change by addressing issues and spreading the organization's message.

To guarantee the change's long-term viability, reinforcement is essential. This includes keeping an eye on developments, acknowledging accomplishments, and adjusting as needed. Leaders can reinforce desired behaviors and create momentum for additional change by praising and rewarding early adopters and others who help the change project succeed. To resolve any lingering issues and guarantee that the change is ingrained in the organization's culture and procedures, it is imperative to maintain open lines of communication and provide continuous feedback.

It is impossible to undervalue the role that technology plays in overcoming opposition to change. Technological developments can help with training, communication, and teamwork, which makes it simpler to initiate and maintain change. Digital platforms, for instance, can give staff members access to online training courses, virtual collaboration tools, and real-time information. These tools help lower uncertainty, increase transparency, and offer continuous assistance during the transition process. Data analytics can also be used to track advancement, spot areas of resistance, and make well-informed judgments on how to handle difficulties.

Fostering an inclusive and diverse culture is a crucial part of overcoming opposition to change. Diverse teams can foster innovation and creativity because they bring a variety of viewpoints and ideas to the table. By making sure that every worker feels acknowledged and appreciated, inclusivity lowers resistance and boosts engagement. Organizations can foster a culture of inclusivity that encourages consideration of varied perspectives and increases employee support for change projects.

In summary, overcoming resistance to change is a difficult task with many facets that call for an all-encompassing strategy. Developing successful methods requires an understanding of the root causes of resistance, which include loss of control, routine disturbance, fear of the unknown, and poor timing. Overcoming resistance requires a combination of crucial elements such as incentives, rewards, support, training, communication, and involvement. The role of leadership is essential in stimulating and encouraging workers, cultivating an environment of transparency and trust, and offering the required backing for effective implementation of changes. Using technology, promoting diversity, and cultivating a culture of adaptation, resilience, and ongoing learning can all help an organization overcome change resistance and succeed in the long run. Organizations may give their employees a positive and long-lasting change experience by using a systematic strategy to change management and promoting the change with ongoing feedback and praise.

CHAPTER IV

Health and Wellness through Kaizen

Physical Fitness

A person who is physically fit may carry out everyday tasks with energy, lower their chance of developing chronic illnesses, and generally improve their quality of life. It includes a number of elements, including flexibility, muscular strength, cardiovascular endurance, and body composition. It takes a combination of consistent exercise, a healthy diet, enough sleep, and mental health to reach and sustain physical fitness. This section examines the value of physical fitness, its advantages for various elements of health, and methods for achieving and maintaining it.

One cannot stress the value of physical fitness given the sedentary lifestyle of today. Many people now lead less physically active lives due to technological improvements, spending a lot of time in front of computers, televisions, and cell phones. Numerous health problems, such as obesity, heart disease, diabetes, and mental health disorders, are exacerbated by this inactivity. These sedentary tendencies are countered by physical fitness, which enhances general health and wellbeing. Physical activity on a regular basis promotes cardiovascular health, muscular strength and endurance, flexibility, and body weight regulation. It also has a significant impact on mental health, lowering stress, anxiety, and depressive symptoms.

The capacity of the heart, lungs, and blood arteries to provide oxygen to working muscles over an extended period of physical activity is known as cardiovascular endurance, and it is one of the main elements of physical fitness. Exercises such as jogging, swimming, cycling, and aerobics improve cardiovascular endurance. By strengthening the heart muscle, enhancing blood circulation, and expanding lung capacity, these exercises lower the risk of heart disease, high blood pressure, and stroke. Frequent cardiovascular activity also raises metabolic rate, which reduces the risk of obesity and helps with weight management.

Both muscular endurance and strength are crucial elements of physical fitness. Muscular endurance is the capacity of a muscle or group of muscles to withstand repeated contractions over an extended period of time. Muscular strength is the ability of a muscle or group of muscles to exert force against resistance. Muscular strength and endurance can be effectively developed by strength training exercises like weightlifting, resistance band exercises, and bodyweight workouts like push-ups and squats. By enhancing bone density, joint health, and general functional fitness, these activities lessen the chance of injury and facilitate daily duties. Improved posture, balance, and coordination are also influenced by increased muscle strength and endurance.

Another essential component of physical fitness is flexibility, which is the range of motion that a joint or collection of joints may achieve. Flexibility-enhancing workouts include Pilates, yoga, and stretching. Increased flexibility eases tense muscles, lowers the chance of injury, and improves general physical performance. It also helps to prevent musculoskeletal diseases and maintain proper posture. Frequent flexibility exercise helps hasten the healing process after physical exertion by easing stiffness and soreness in the muscles.

The last element of physical fitness, body composition, describes the proportions of lean and fat mass in the body. Regular physical exercise combined with a well-balanced diet can help maintain a good body composition, which is crucial for general health. A higher risk of chronic illnesses, such as diabetes, heart disease, and some types of cancer, is linked to excess body fat. Conversely, a higher percentage of lean mass is associated with enhanced strength, increased physical functionality, and better metabolic health.

Beyond just improving physical health, physical fitness has a profound effect on mental and emotional wellness. Frequent exercise has been demonstrated to boost mood, strengthen cognitive abilities, and lessen the signs of anxiety and sadness. Endorphins are neurotransmitters that are released in response to physical activity and are known to enhance emotions of happiness and wellbeing. Additionally, it lowers cortisol levels, which helps to relieve tension and encourage relaxation. Furthermore, exercise has been connected to better sleep, which is crucial for both physical and mental well-being.

Participating in physical exercise can also improve social well-being. Engaging in recreational activities, sports, and group workouts offers chances for social interaction and the formation of social support networks. These exchanges can improve overall life satisfaction, strengthen a sense of community, and lessen feelings of isolation and loneliness. Participating in physical activities helps kids and teenagers build their leadership, cooperation, and social skills, all of which benefit their general growth and wellbeing.

Maintaining physical fitness necessitates a multifaceted strategy that includes regular exercise, a healthy diet, enough sleep, and mental health. The American Heart Association suggests engaging in muscle-strengthening activities two or more days a week in addition to 150 minutes of moderate-intensity aerobic activity or 75 minutes of vigorous-intensity aerobic activity per week. Selecting sustainable and pleasurable activities is crucial since it improves the chances of sticking to a regular fitness schedule.

A balanced diet is essential to physical fitness because it supplies the energy and nutrients needed to maintain both physical exercise and general health. A diverse range of foods, such as fruits, vegetables, whole grains, lean meats, and healthy fats, should be a part of any balanced diet. Sufficient hydration is also necessary for the best possible physical performance and recuperation. Foods high in nutrients assist muscle growth and repair, provide you with the energy you need to exercise and improve your general health and wellbeing.

Recuperation and adequate rest are essential parts of a physical fitness program. The body uses rest to rebuild and repair tissues, recuperate from physical activity, and guard against overtraining and injuries. The National Sleep Foundation recommends that individuals get between seven and nine hours of quality sleep every night in order to maintain good physical and mental health. Enhancing physical performance and general health can be achieved by incorporating rest days into an exercise regimen and maintaining proper sleep hygiene.

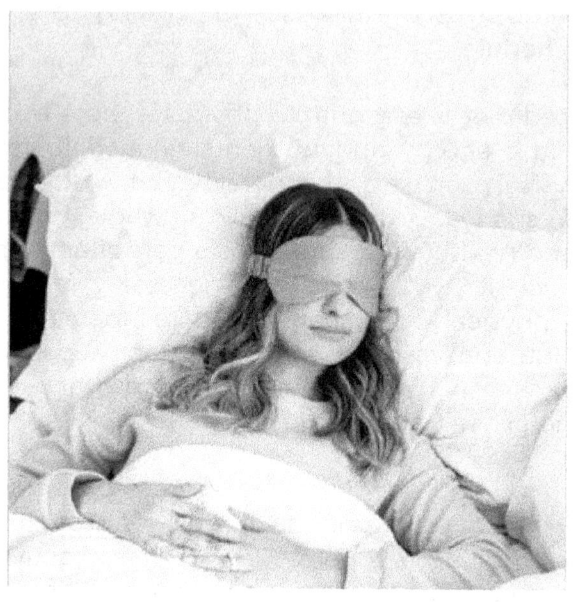

Physical fitness and mental well-being are closely related, and stress reduction and an optimistic outlook are critical to general health. Deep breathing exercises and other mindfulness-based activities can ease tension and encourage calm. Creating attainable fitness objectives and acknowledging accomplishments can increase self-confidence and drive. It's critical to understand that achieving physical fitness is a journey and that long-term success depends on keeping a good outlook and committing to healthy behaviors.

Adding fun and diversity to a physical exercise regimen can improve compliance and overall pleasure. Discovering new forms of exercise, like dance, hiking, or martial arts, can add excitement and enjoyment to the routine. Participating in recreational sports teams or fitness programs can offer social contact and inspiration. Exercise can be made more pleasurable and fulfilling by adding new tasks, working out with a friend, or listening to music.

Prior to beginning a new fitness program, it is crucial for people with physical limitations or chronic health concerns to speak with healthcare specialists. Physical fitness can be safely attained with the aid of individualized training programs that take into account each person's health, talents, and goals. In order to guarantee that physical fitness is acquired and maintained in a safe manner, healthcare professionals can provide advice on suitable exercises, adjustments, and safety measures.

Environmental and community variables are also crucial in encouraging physical fitness. Physical activity can be promoted by having access to parks, walking paths, and safe, reasonably priced recreational facilities. Fitness courses, wellness programs, and organized sports leagues are a few examples of community-based projects and programs that encourage active living and can help people reach their fitness objectives. Developing surroundings that support active commuting, including cycling and walking, can help raise levels of physical activity.

Technology is playing a bigger and bigger part in encouraging physical fitness. Tools for recording physical activity, creating objectives, and keeping track of progress are available through fitness applications, wearable technology, and internet platforms. With the help of these technologies, people may maintain their motivation and engagement more easily by receiving individualized exercise regimens, online coaching, and social support. Even in situations when in-person activities are not feasible, virtual fitness clubs and online classes offer chances for accountability and connection.

Promoting physical fitness in the workplace and in schools can enhance productivity and health outcomes. Enhancing physical and mental well-being can be achieved through putting physical education programs into place, promoting active breaks, and offering opportunities for physical activity. Workplaces can encourage physical fitness by providing fitness centers, wellness initiatives, and rewards for walking or jogging to work. For both individuals and communities, fostering a culture of health and well-being in work and educational environments can have long-term advantages.

To sum up, physical fitness is a complex and vital component of general health and wellbeing. It includes body composition, physical strength, muscular endurance, flexibility, and cardiovascular endurance. Maintaining physical fitness necessitates a multifaceted strategy that includes regular exercise, a healthy diet, enough sleep, and mental health. Beyond just improving one's physical health, physical fitness has a profound effect on one's cognitive, emotional, and social wellbeing. Selecting pleasurable activities, adding diversity, establishing reasonable goals, and enlisting the aid of medical professionals and community resources are some strategies for achieving and maintaining physical fitness. People can lower their chance of developing chronic illnesses, improve their quality of life, and feel more fulfilled and well-being by adopting a lifestyle that places a high priority on physical fitness.

Mental Wellness

The concept of mental wellbeing is complex and includes social, psychological, and emotional well-being. It has an impact on people's thoughts, feelings, and behaviors, which in turn influences how they manage stress, interact with others, and make decisions. It is imperative that mental health be maintained throughout life, from childhood to adulthood. Despite its significance, mental wellbeing is frequently disregarded or misinterpreted, which can result in a number of mental health problems. This paper examines the importance of mental health, the variables that affect it, the effects of disregarding it, and methods to improve and preserve mental health.

It is impossible to overestimate the importance of mental wellbeing because it is essential to general health and life satisfaction. Good connections, efficient stress management, high self-esteem, and the capacity to overcome obstacles in life are all correlated with mental wellness. It makes it possible for people to work effectively, reach their full potential, and meaningfully impact their communities. Poor mental health, on the other hand, can result in a variety of issues, including mental disorders like substance misuse, depression, and anxiety, which can have a negative influence on a person's life as well as the lives of people around them.

Mental wellbeing is influenced by a number of variables, including social, psychological, and biological ones. Genetics, brain chemistry, and physical health issues are examples of biological influences. Life experiences, coping mechanisms, and personality traits are examples of psychological elements. Relationships, cultural influences, and socioeconomic position are all considered social variables. Comprehending these variables is essential in formulating efficacious approaches to foster psychological well-being and tackle psychological disorders.

Mental health is significantly influenced by biological variables. Certain mental health disorders, such as depression, bipolar disorder, and schizophrenia, can be inherited by an individual. Because abnormalities in neurotransmitters like serotonin, dopamine, and norepinephrine can cause mood disorders and other mental health problems, brain chemistry also has an impact on mental wellness. Physical health issues that impair an individual's quality of life, such as chronic disease or injury, can also have an effect on mental wellness by generating stress, suffering, and limits. Understanding the relationship between biological variables and mental health is crucial for recognizing and treating mental health problems.

Equal weight is given to psychological variables in determining mental wellbeing. Resilience, optimism, and self-efficacy are examples of personality traits that can improve mental health and enable people to deal with stress and hardship. On the other hand, characteristics that lead to poor mental health include perfectionism, low self-esteem, and pessimism. The acquisition of coping abilities through social interactions and life experiences is essential for stress management and mental wellbeing maintenance. Efficient coping mechanisms, such as problem-solving, reaching out to others for support, and practicing relaxation techniques, can lessen the adverse effects of stress and enhance mental health. Maladaptive coping mechanisms, on the other hand, such as substance abuse, self-harm, and avoidance, can make mental health problems worse.

Social factors, such as socioeconomic level, cultural influences, and the quality of one's connections, have a substantial impact on mental wellness. Good connections with friends, family, and coworkers offer chances for social interaction, a sense of belonging, and emotional support —all of which are beneficial to mental health. In contrast, loneliness, despair, and anxiety can result from toxic relationships, social isolation, and a lack of social support. Individuals' perceptions and reactions to mental health difficulties are shaped by cultural influences on ideas, values, and attitudes regarding mental health. Discrimination and stigma around mental health might discourage people from getting treatment and make them feel even more alone and ashamed. Because it determines one's ability to access resources like healthcare, education, and work possibilities, socioeconomic status has an impact on mental wellness. Living in impoverished neighborhoods, experiencing financial instability, and being unemployed can all raise stress levels and the likelihood of mental health issues.

Neglecting mental health can have detrimental effects on people as well as society. Numerous harmful effects, such as decreased functioning, a lower quality of life, and a higher chance of physical health issues, are linked to poor mental health. Anxiety and depression are examples of mental health conditions that can make it challenging to go about daily tasks, which can have an impact on relationships, employment, and education. People who are mentally ill are more likely to participate in risky activities, including drug misuse, self-harm, and suicidal thoughts and actions. The financial toll that mental health problems take is significant, involving expenses for social services, healthcare, and lost productivity. In addition, a low mental state can lead to broken families, strained relationships, and higher rates of criminality.

A comprehensive strategy that includes community involvement, professional support, and self-care is required to improve and preserve mental wellness. Self-care techniques, which include leading a healthy lifestyle, controlling stress, cultivating wholesome relationships, and partaking in wellbeing-promoting activities, are essential to mental wellness. For good physical and mental health, one must practice mindfulness and meditation, eat a balanced diet, get enough sleep, and engage in regular physical activity. Identifying stressors, coming up with proper coping mechanisms, and designing a balanced lifestyle that allows for work, play, and relaxation are all part of managing stress. Good connections offer chances for social interaction, a sense of belonging, and emotional support. Empathy, respect for one another, and efficient communication are all necessary for establishing and sustaining successful partnerships. By giving one a sense of purpose, contentment, and joy, hobbies, artistic endeavors, and volunteer work are examples of well-being-promoting activities that can improve mental wellness.

It is imperative that those who are facing mental health concerns receive professional treatment. Psychologists, psychiatrists, counselors, and social workers are examples of mental health professionals who offer mental health condition assessment, diagnosis, and treatment. Psychotherapy, also referred to as talk therapy, is a valuable treatment for a number of mental health conditions, including trauma, anxiety, and depression. Various therapeutic approaches, such as dialectical behavior therapy (DBT), psychodynamic therapy, and cognitive-behavioral therapy (CBT), can assist people in comprehending and controlling their ideas, feelings, and actions. A psychiatrist or other medical professional's prescription medication may be a crucial part of the treatment for mental health issues like schizophrenia, bipolar disorder, and depression. Medication can assist in controlling brain chemistry, reduce symptoms, and enhance performance. It frequently works best when paired with other supportive interventions, such as psychotherapy.

Participation in the community is essential for fostering mental wellness as well. Communities are important because they create social environments and support networks that help people maintain mental health. Mental wellness can benefit from community programs and initiatives that lower stigma, increase mental health awareness, and offer resources and support. Employers, community organizations, and schools can all foster mental health by enacting mental health-promoting policies and procedures, such as mental health education, employee assistance programs, and anti-bullying initiatives. People can connect with people who have gone through similar things, offer emotional support, and exchange resources and information through social networks and support groups. Participating in the community can promote a feeling of purpose, social responsibility, and belonging, all of which are beneficial to mental health.

Promoting mental wellbeing and averting mental health problems require preventive strategies. For those who are at risk, early intervention and prevention techniques can improve results and lower the likelihood that they will experience mental health issues. Early intervention can be facilitated, and those at risk of mental health difficulties can be identified with the use of screening and assessment tools. Programs for education and awareness can lower stigma, promote help-seeking behaviors, and broaden people's knowledge and comprehension of mental health. Developing resilience via courses that cover stress reduction, emotional control, and coping mechanisms can assist people in overcoming obstacles in life and preserving their mental health. By teaching kids and teenagers how to control their emotions, form wholesome relationships, and make responsible decisions, social and emotional learning (SEL) programs in schools can support mental wellness.

In addition, public structures and policies are essential for advancing mental wellness. By providing financing for mental health services, putting in place initiatives to promote mental health, and passing laws addressing social determinants of mental health like housing, education, and poverty, governments, and legislators may assist mental health. Laws requiring insurance providers to cover mental and physical health disorders equally might increase access to mental health services. These laws are known as mental health parity laws. By offering complete and all-encompassing care, integrating mental health services into primary care settings can improve access to mental health treatment and lessen stigma. In order to advance mental health and guarantee that decisions about public policy and funding give priority to mental health issues, advocacy, and activism are crucial. In order to enhance mental wellness, advocacy initiatives can lessen stigma, increase awareness, and encourage systemic changes.

To sum up, mental wellness is an essential component of total health and wellbeing, which includes social, psychological, and emotional well-being. A complicated interaction between biological, psychological, and social variables influences it. A comprehensive strategy that incorporates professional assistance, self-care, and community involvement is needed to maintain mental wellness. Neglecting mental health can have detrimental effects on people's functioning, quality of life, and likelihood of developing physical health issues, among other effects on society as a whole. Advocating for legislation that supports mental health, participating in community activities, obtaining professional support, and practicing self-care are some strategies to improve and sustain mental wellness. People who prioritize their mental health can live longer, make a positive impact on their communities, and face obstacles head-on with courage and perseverance.

Nutrition

A vital component of human health and wellbeing is nutrition, which includes consuming and using nutrients to maintain life and advance maximum health. It is essential for healthy development, sickness prevention, and general life quality. Studying nutrition entails learning about the roles played by different nutrients, the effects of dietary decisions on health, and the fundamentals of a balanced diet. This section explores the importance of nutrition, the body's need for certain essential nutrients, the connection between diet and health, and methods for obtaining and preserving adequate nutrition.

Nutrition is more important than just giving us the energy we need to go about our daily lives. For newborns and children to grow and develop normally, for the body to maintain its functions, and to avoid chronic disorders, proper nutrition is crucial. The building blocks of the organism, nutrients play a role in the composition and operation of tissues, cells, and organs. They are essential for immunological response, metabolism, and tissue upkeep and repair in the body. The maintenance of life and the promotion of health depend on a diet that is well-balanced and supplies all necessary nutrients in the right amounts.

The six main classes of essential nutrients are water, vitamins, minerals, proteins, fats, and carbs. Every one of these nutrients has a specific purpose in the body and is essential to good health. The body uses carbohydrates as its primary energy source. Foods like grains, fruits, vegetables, and legumes contain them. Glucose, the product of breaking down carbohydrates, is utilized by cells as an energy source. Carbohydrates come in two varieties: simple carbohydrates, which are sugars, and complex carbs, which include starches and fiber. Complex carbs break down more slowly than simple carbohydrates, giving them a longer-lasting energy boost and improving digestive health.

Body tissues require proteins for growth, maintenance, and repair. They consist of amino acids, some of which must be received through diet as they are necessary. Meat, chicken, fish, eggs, dairy products, legumes, nuts, and seeds are examples of foods high in protein. Building and repairing muscles, enzymes, hormones, and other bodily structures depend heavily on proteins. They also aid in immune system support and physiological process regulation.

Fats are essential for the absorption of fat-soluble vitamins (A, D, E, and K) and are a concentrated source of energy. They also aid in maintaining cell membranes, insulating the body, and safeguarding organs. Fats come in a variety of forms, such as trans, unsaturated, and saturated fats. Foods high in unsaturated fats, such avocados, nuts, seeds, and olive oil, are suitable for your heart. On the other hand, because they are linked to a higher risk of heart disease, saturated and trans fats, which are present in processed foods, fatty meats, and dairy products, should be consumed in moderation.

Vitamins are organic substances that are necessary for the body's numerous metabolic functions. They must come from the food and are needed in tiny amounts. Vitamins can be divided into two groups: fat-soluble vitamins (such as vitamins A, D, E, and K) and water-soluble vitamins (like vitamin C and B vitamins). Vitamins are necessary for the synthesis of energy, immunological response, blood coagulation, and the preservation of good skin and vision. A diversified diet is essential to getting all the vitamins you need because each vitamin has a distinct function and can be found in a variety of foods.

Inorganic elements known as minerals are necessary for a number of physiological processes. They consist of trace minerals, including iron, zinc, copper, manganese, iodine, selenium, and fluoride, as well as macrominerals like calcium, phosphorus, magnesium, sodium, potassium, chloride, and sulfur. Minerals play a role in supporting healthy neuron and muscle function, controlling metabolism, and forming strong bones and teeth. A vast variety of foods, such as dairy products, meat, fish, fruits, vegetables, and cereals, contain them.

One of the nutrients that is necessary for life is water. It comprises a sizable amount of the body and is essential to several processes, such as controlling body temperature, moving nutrients and waste materials, and preserving fluid equilibrium. Maintaining proper hydration is necessary for good health, and the amount of water the body needs depends on a number of variables, including age, gender, degree of exercise, and ambient conditions.

Many studies have established the connection between nutrition and health, showing how dietary decisions affect the likelihood of developing chronic illnesses as well as general health outcomes. Obesity, diabetes, heart disease, and some types of cancer are among the chronic diseases that are linked to a lower risk of eating a balanced diet rich in nutrient-dense foods. On the other hand, lousy eating patterns, such as a diet heavy in processed foods, sugar-filled drinks, and harmful fats, might hasten the onset of chronic illnesses.

Diet has a significant impact on heart disease, the world's most prominent cause of mortality. Atherosclerosis, hypertension, and elevated cholesterol levels are some of the ways that diets heavy in saturated and trans fats, cholesterol, and sodium can raise the risk of heart disease. On the other side, by lowering blood pressure, improving lipid profiles, and reducing inflammation, diets high in fruits, vegetables, whole grains, lean meats, and healthy fats can support heart health.

Dietary practices are closely associated with diabetes, especially type 2 diabetes. Diets heavy in sugary foods, processed carbs, and unhealthy fats can aggravate insulin resistance and cause type 2 diabetes. On the other hand, diets that prioritize fiber, lean meats, whole grains, and healthy fats can lower the risk of diabetes and help control blood sugar levels.

Nutrition and physical activity both have an impact on obesity, a serious public health issue. Sedentary lifestyles coupled with high-calorie, low-nutrient meals are a significant cause of weight gain and obesity. Heart disease, diabetes, and some types of cancer are among the chronic diseases that obesity increases the risk of developing. For optimal weight management and general health, adopting a balanced diet that prioritizes nutrient-dense foods and portion control is crucial. Regular physical activity is also recommended.

Dietary factors also impact some types of cancer. An increased risk of colorectal cancer is linked to diets low in fruits, vegetables, and fiber and heavy in alcohol, red meats, and processed meats. Because plant-based foods, whole grains, and healthy fats contain antioxidants, fiber, and other bioactive chemicals that guard against cellular damage and inflammation, eating a diet high in these foods can help lower the risk of developing different malignancies.

A comprehensive strategy that takes into account each person's requirements, preferences, and lifestyle circumstances is necessary to achieve and maintain optimal nutrition. Three critical components of a balanced diet are proportionality, moderation, and diversity. Eating a variety of foods is one way to make sure you get all the nutrients you need. A diversified diet helps to prevent vitamin deficits and enhances general health since different foods contain different amounts of nutrients.

In order to prevent ingesting too many calories, sugar, fat, or sodium, moderation refers to consuming meals and liquids in reasonable proportions. It is crucial to strike a balance between eating a lot of nutrient-dense foods and occasionally indulging in less nutritious options. In addition, moderation entails mindful eating techniques including observing indications of hunger and fullness and abstaining from overindulging.

In order to achieve nutritional needs, proportionality entails balancing the intake of various food categories. A diet rich in fruits, vegetables, whole grains, lean proteins, and healthy fats is advised by the Dietary Guidelines for Americans. A substantial amount of the diet should consist of fruits and vegetables since they are good sources of vitamins, minerals, fiber, and antioxidants. Because whole grains include more fiber and minerals than refined grains, they are recommended. Examples of whole grains include brown rice, quinoa, and whole wheat bread.

Lean protein sources such as fish, poultry, beans, lentils, and tofu are essential for both general health and muscle upkeep and repair. Nuts, seeds, avocados, and olive oil are good sources of healthy fats that are vital for heart health and general well-being. Limiting the consumption of sodium added sugars, trans fats, and saturated and trans fats—all of which are frequently present in processed and fast food—is crucial.

Planning and preparing meals can assist people in achieving and maintaining appropriate nutrition. Meal planning in advance can help avoid impulsive, unhealthy food choices and allows for careful assessment of dietary needs. Meal preparation at home gives you more control over item selection, cooking techniques, and portion sizes since it uses fresh and minimally processed ingredients. Involving family members in meal preparation and planning has additional advantages, such as promoting good eating habits and offering chances for connection and education.

In order to encourage healthy eating practices and prevent diet-related diseases, nutrition education and awareness are essential. In order to provide nutrition instruction and resources, community organizations, school programs, and public health efforts are crucial. People may take charge of their health by learning the advantages of a balanced diet, how to read food labels, and how to make good food choices. In addition, nutrition education ought to tackle the cultural and socioeconomic determinants of dietary practices, offering workable and affordable solutions to a range of demographics.

Improving nutrition and health outcomes requires addressing food security and access to wholesome foods. Millions of people worldwide experience food insecurity, which is characterized as having insufficient or unpredictable access to enough food and is linked to poor nutrition and unfavorable health effects. Increasing the accessibility and cost of nutritious meals, assisting regional food systems, and offering nutrition support services to disadvantaged groups are all steps toward enhancing food security. Initiatives like food coops, farmers' markets, and community gardens can improve access to wholesome, fresh food.

Government policy and initiatives play a significant influence in advancing public health and nutrition. Policies that encourage healthy eating can be put in place by governments. Some of these include controlling food labeling, prohibiting the marketing of harmful foods to minors, and offering financial rewards for the production and consumption of nutritious foods. Nutrition education and awareness programs run by public health organizations can help improve dietary practices and health outcomes. Governments, healthcare providers, community organizations, and the food business must work together to create an environment that promotes optimal nutrition and healthy eating.

In summary, nutrition refers to the consumption and application of vital nutrients and is an essential component of health and wellness. For healthy growth and development, disease prevention, and general life quality, proper nutrition is essential. To give the body the nutrition it needs to function at its best, a balanced diet with a range of nutrient-dense foods is crucial. It is commonly known that diet and health are related, with poor eating habits causing chronic illness development and ideal nutrition fostering health and long life. A comprehensive strategy that takes into account each person's requirements, preferences, and lifestyle circumstances is necessary to achieve and maintain optimal nutrition. In order to encourage good eating practices and prevent diet-related diseases, it is imperative that people have access to nutritious foods, education, and awareness. Individuals and communities can strive toward achieving optimal nutrition and enhancing public health through cooperative efforts and supporting policies.

CHAPTER V

Kaizen in Relationships and Communication

Improving Personal Relationships

One of the most important aspects of raising emotional wellbeing and improving life quality is improving interpersonal interactions. Whether platonic, familial, or romantic, relationships are essential for offering companionship, support, and a feeling of identity. However, it takes ongoing work, comprehension, and communication to preserve and strengthen these relationships. This section examines the value of interpersonal relationships, the typical difficulties they encounter, and methods for fostering and enhancing these bonds to keep them happy and healthy.

Human life and well-being are fundamentally dependent on interpersonal relationships. They give us emotional support, guide us through the difficulties of life, and enhance our satisfaction and sense of value. Stronger emotional and physical connections can result in happier moods, reduced stress, and better mental and physical health. On the other hand, a lackluster or tense relationship might exacerbate depressive, anxious, and lonely sensations. For this reason, knowing how to establish and preserve healthy relationships is crucial to general wellbeing.

Effective communication is one of the cornerstones of building better personal relationships. People communicate by exchanging information, expressing their emotions, and making their needs and wants known to one another. It entails speaking as well as attentive, sympathetic listening. Active listening entails giving the speaker your undivided attention, comprehending what they're saying, and meaningfully answering. It involves acknowledging the sentiments of the other person, avoiding interruptions, and demonstrating empathy. People are more likely to feel appreciated and respected when they are heard and understood, which improves the relationship.

Another essential element of wholesome partnerships is empathy. Empathy is recognizing and comprehending the thoughts, feelings, and viewpoints of another person by placing oneself in their position. It calls for compassion and open-mindedness even when we disagree with the other person's point of view. Since empathy demonstrates our concern and appreciation for the feelings and experiences of others, it fosters connection and trust. Empathy exercises can result in more meaningful interactions and deeper bonds.

Any relationship will inevitably experience conflict. However, the way disagreement is handled can have a significant effect on the relationship's wellbeing. In order to resolve conflicts constructively, parties must cooperate and treat one another with respect. It necessitates avoiding placing blame, maintaining composure, and concentrating on coming up with compromises. Active listening and "I" statements are two strategies that can help defuse tensions and advance understanding. "I" comments convey emotions without placing blame on the other party. It's crucial to know when to stop talking if feelings get too intense and to pick up the conversation again when everyone has calmed down.

Any healthy relationship is built on trust. Honesty, dependability, and consistency are necessary to establish and preserve confidence. Over time, trust is built via behaviors that exhibit dedication, reliability, and honesty. Although it might be difficult to rebuild trust once it has been damaged, it is possible with honest apologies, accepting accountability for acts, and showing that you are genuinely trying to alter your behavior. Both sides must be patient and forgiving in order to rebuild trust.

Having healthy relationships requires setting and upholding limits. Boundaries are the restrictions we place on what constitutes acceptable behavior in our relationships with other people. They guarantee that our needs and ideals are upheld and contribute to safeguarding our mental and physical health. Setting and maintaining limits in an authoritative yet non-aggressive manner is essential. Respecting other people's boundaries is equally vital. Set healthy boundaries to avoid anger and exhaustion while fostering respect for one another.

An essential component of any personal relationship is mutual respect. Respect entails appreciating one another's needs, wants, and viewpoints. It involves being considerate and polite to one another even when there is disagreement. Respectful conduct creates a happy, encouraging atmosphere where everyone feels appreciated and understood. It also entails acknowledging and valuing each other's unique traits and contributions.

Spending quality time together is essential to fostering connections. Stronger links and enduring memories can be made by sharing experiences, having meaningful conversations, and partaking in activities that both sides like. Time spent together should always come first, even with hectic schedules and other obligations. Maintaining intimacy and connection can be facilitated by making time for regular social interactions, such as movie evenings, get-togethers with family, or informal get-togethers with friends.

Developing forgiveness is essential to enhancing interpersonal connections. Intimacy and understanding can be hampered by holding onto grudges and past wrongs. To be forgiven is to let go of grudges and look forward to the future with optimism. It means deciding to let go of the bad feelings connected to harmful behavior, not endorsing it. Growth and healing can result from forgiveness, both personally and in a partnership.

Developing one's self-awareness and self-care is equally crucial for strengthening interpersonal bonds. Being aware of our own needs, feelings, and triggers can improve our ability to communicate and handle conflict. Maintaining a healthy lifestyle, controlling stress, and pursuing interests outside of work are examples of self-care practices that guarantee we have the mental and physical stamina to devote to our relationships. We are better able to assist and relate to others when we look after ourselves.

Expressing gratitude and admiration is a crucial part of strengthening personal ties. Stronger links and a more positive atmosphere can be created by expressing thanks for the good things in the relationship and recognizing the efforts and attributes of the other person. Making the other person feel appreciated and loved can be accomplished in large part by small acts of kindness, words of affirmation, and expressions of gratitude.

Additionally essential to strengthening interpersonal bonds is vulnerability. A stronger sense of connection and trust can be fostered by discussing our hopes, worries, and uncertainties with others. Being vulnerable entails accepting the prospect of rejection or criticism as well as taking emotional risks. But it also makes real intimacy and comprehension possible. In relationships, there is a sense of safety and acceptance when both people are willing to be vulnerable.

Healthy relationships require flexibility and the ability to adjust to change. Relationships can be impacted by external forces, personal development, and life situations. Navigating these obstacles and preserving a solid connection can be facilitated by being flexible and open to change. Being adaptable means lowering standards, making concessions, and encouraging one another through changes.

One of the most important aspects of personal relationships is support during hard times. During trying times, offering moral, practical, and emotional assistance can show commitment and caring and improve relationships. It entails being there, lending a sympathetic ear, and providing assistance when required. During trying circumstances, comfort and assurance can be given by demonstrating empathy and understanding.

Ultimately, strengthening interpersonal ties requires getting expert assistance when necessary. For resolving relationship problems, therapy or counseling can offer insightful information, practical skills, and effective approaches. Specialist advice can assist in determining the root causes of issues, enhancing communication, and creating more positive interaction patterns. In order to maintain and strengthen healthy relationships, asking for assistance is a proactive move.

In summary, strengthening interpersonal ties is a complex process that calls for work, patience, and dedication. Crucial components of fostering and improving personal relationships include effective communication, empathy, conflict resolution, trust, boundaries, mutual respect, quality time, forgiveness, self-awareness, appreciation, vulnerability, flexibility, support, and expert assistance. People can build and sustain meaningful and healthful relationships that improve their general well-being and quality of life by making investments in these areas. Improving relationships can result in increased pleasure, fulfillment, and emotional well-being because they are an essential aspect of the human experience.

Effective Communication adjustments

Proficiency in communication is a crucial ability in both private and work environments. It makes understanding easier, builds relationships, and makes problem-solving and teamwork possible. For communication to be clear and compelling, it must be modified to fit various settings, audiences, and goals. This section examines the many facets of good communication changes, such as embracing technology in communication, comprehending diverse communication styles cultural concerns, adapting to varied circumstances, and using non-verbal communication.

Making improvements to communication that works requires first understanding diverse communication styles. People communicate in a variety of methods that are shaped by their choices, backgrounds, and personalities. Some people prefer to speak in a clear and succinct manner and are straightforward and assertive.

Others might be more subtly expressive, appreciating balance and nuance in their relationships. It is possible to avoid misunderstandings and promote more fruitful conversations by acknowledging these distinctions and modifying one's communication style accordingly. In a professional environment, for example, a manager may need to take a more authoritative posture when providing instructions and then change to a more sympathetic stance when attending to an employee's personal issues.

Effective communication also requires careful awareness of cultural differences. Cultural conventions, values, and communication techniques vary widely. In one culture, something may be viewed as courteous and respectful in a different way. For instance, maintaining direct eye contact may be viewed as aggressive or impolite in certain cultures, but it may also be a sign of confidence and honesty in others. Likewise, different cultures interpret gestures, body language, and even silence differently. Cultural sensitivity and awareness are prerequisites for effective communication since they allow one to modify their message to fit the expectations of the audience. This could entail being aware of non-verbal clues, speaking in a way that is appropriate for the culture of one's clients or coworkers, and learning about their cultural background.

Another essential component of suitable communication modifications is context adaptation. Different communication strategies are needed in other settings. For example, professional contexts like business meetings or academic presentations usually need formal communication. This entails speaking intelligibly and succinctly, following formal procedures, and acting in a polished manner. However, informal communication is better suited for more relaxed and conversational settings, such as get-togethers with friends or family. It is easier to make sure that the message is received favorably and successfully when the context is understood, and communication is adjusted correctly.

Effective communication modifications heavily rely on nonverbal communication. More effectively than words, non-verbal clues, including posture, eye contact, gestures, and facial expressions, can indicate emotions and intentions. Skilled communicators are aware of these indicators and modify their body language to support their spoken words. For example, keeping eye contact conveys attention and attentiveness, and a warm smile fosters connection and trust. On the other hand, poor eye contact or crossed arms might obstruct communication. Effective communication requires both being aware of one's own nonverbal cues and effectively reading those of others.

With the introduction of new platforms and technologies that call for particular communication modifications, technology has completely changed the way we communicate. Effective communication in the modern digital age frequently entails the use of social media, video conferencing, messaging applications, and email. Every one of these platforms has customs and best practices unique to it. For example, emails should be formatted correctly, have a professional tone, and be clear and succinct. It's essential to pay attention to both visual and auditory aspects of video conferencing, such as speaking effectively, keeping eye contact with the camera, and turning down background noise. Conversely, communication through social media frequently takes a more casual and participatory style. It is possible to improve communication and guarantee that the desired message is successfully communicated by adjusting to these various platforms and employing them effectively.

A crucial element of good communication is active listening, which frequently needs modification. To actively listen, one must give their whole attention to the speaker, comprehend what they are saying, and give a considered response. It calls for patience, empathy, and focus. Enhancing listening abilities to fit various situations and people can significantly improve communication results. To guarantee understanding, active listening in a team meeting could entail asking clarifying questions and summarizing important information. To provide support and knowledge in a personal interaction, it could be necessary to convey empathy and validation. By adapting listening techniques to the speaker's needs and the circumstances at hand, communicators can promote mutual respect and stronger relationships.

For communication to be effective, it must be concise and clear. Being detailed, avoiding needless jargon, and rationally organizing the message are all part of making communication plain and succinct. This is especially crucial in work environments because precise and unambiguous communication can boost output and avoid miscommunications. For instance, a manager should avoid using vague terminology and instead offer precise, step-by-step instructions to a team. Similar to this, brief paragraphs, headings, and bullet points can all improve the effectiveness of information conveyed in written communication. Making communication more succinct and clear guarantees that the message is grasped and acted upon.

Another essential component of successful communication modifications is empathy. Empathy is the capacity to comprehend and experience another person's emotions. It fosters the development of rapport, trust, and emotional ties. In order to change communication to be more sympathetic, one must actively listen, validate the sentiments of the other person, and react compassionately. This is especially crucial when the other person is under stress, dissatisfaction, or emotional suffering. In a customer service capacity, for instance, empathetically addressing an irate client can assist in defusing the issue and achieving a mutually agreeable outcome. Similar to this, sympathetic communication can improve mutual understanding and fortify ties in interpersonal interactions.

Effective communication depends on feedback, which needs to be carefully adjusted. Effective feedback-giving and -receiving requires being specific, considerate, and constructive. Feedback can be more successful if it is tailored to the recipient's preferences, personality, and situation. For example, although some people respond better to a more soft and sympathetic approach, others may prefer plain and unambiguous comments. Another critical factor is timing; giving comments as soon as possible after an event can have a more significant effect than waiting. Furthermore, fostering an atmosphere of safety and support when receiving feedback promotes transparency and openness. A culture of ongoing development and progress can be encouraged by modifying criticism to be kind and constructive.

Developing self-awareness is essential to improving communication. Understanding one's own communication style, areas of strength, and room for development enables people to adjust to various audiences and circumstances more skillfully. Self-awareness entails asking for feedback from others, thinking back on previous communication encounters, and remaining receptive to new information and development. For instance, someone who is aware of their propensity to dominate talks should deliberately try to listen more and give other people an opportunity to speak. In a similar vein, someone who is often too critical of others may want to focus on providing more fair and helpful criticism. Through self-awareness and proactive adjustment, communicators can improve their efficacy and forge stronger bonds with others.

It's crucial to modify communication for various age groups. When it comes to communication, different age groups could have other requirements, expectations, and preferences. Younger people, for example, could favor more casual and technologically aware forms of communication like social media or texting. Conversely, older people may prefer more formal or face-to-face communication methods. Bridging generational gaps and ensuring a positive reception of the message can be achieved by acknowledging these preferences and tailoring communication accordingly. For instance, being patient, speaking intelligibly, and avoiding jargon are all ways to build connection and comprehension while interacting with senior citizens.

Effective communication in professional environments requires adapting to various roles and hierarchies. Depending on a person's role and position within an organization, communication styles and expectations might differ significantly. For example, speaking with senior executives may call for a more formal, succinct style that emphasizes important details and results. Conversely, talking with colleagues or subordinates could facilitate a more thorough and cooperative conversation. It may be ensured that the message is communicated appropriately and effectively by having an understanding of the expectations and communication styles associated with various positions and hierarchies. For instance, it can be more successful in highlighting high-level accomplishments and strategic consequences rather than going into technical specifics when providing a project update to senior management.

Another crucial factor to take into account is adapting communication to suit various learning styles. Individuals receive and comprehend information in different ways; visual, auditory, and kinesthetic learning styles are often used to categorize these methods. Information given in textual, charted, and diagrammatic formats is preferred by visual learners. Spoken explanations and debates are beneficial for auditory learners. The best learning methods for kinesthetic learners are practical exercises and encounters. Understanding these variations and adapting communication to accommodate different learning styles helps improve comprehension and participation. For instance, in a training session, mixing interactive exercises, spoken explanations, and visual aids can accommodate various learning styles and guarantee that the material is conveyed clearly.

Effective communication modifications must include addressing communication hurdles. Language obstacles, physical impairments, mental barriers, and technical difficulties are a few examples of communication impediments. To overcome these obstacles, one must be flexible and have innovative problem-solving skills. For example, translation services, visual aids, and primary language can all help close the gap when language barriers are present. Using assistive technology, textual communication, or sign language interpreters can improve understanding while interacting with those who have hearing loss. In order to overcome emotional obstacles, it may be necessary to establish a secure and encouraging atmosphere where people feel free to express themselves. Encouraging everyone to completely and effectively participate in the communication process means being proactive in recognizing and resolving communication impediments.

Developing rapport and trust is essential to communicating effectively. Building a rapport with the audience based on mutual trust can improve communication and increase the effectiveness of modifications. Finding common ground, being respectful, and demonstrating genuine interest are all necessary for developing rapport. It calls for endurance, attentive hearing, and compassion. Over time, trust is developed via dependable and constant communication.

Restructuring communication to be more open, sincere, and encouraging can aid in establishing and preserving trust. In a team environment, for instance, providing regular updates on team members' progress, recognizing their efforts, and being receptive to criticism can all help to build trust and foster collaboration.

It's also critical to modify communication to accommodate varying emotional states. Emotional states have a significant influence on how people receive and react to communication. Understanding these emotional states and changing one's communication style might improve efficacy. Giving someone a calm, collected response while they're angry or stressed, for instance, can assist defuse the situation. Conversely, when someone is eager or ecstatic, mirroring their energy.

Conflict Resolution

The ability to resolve conflicts is crucial in both personal and professional contexts. It entails having the skill to effectively handle and settle disputes while making sure that everyone involved feels heard, respected, and satisfied with the solution. Given the diversity of viewpoints, interests, and values, conflicts will inevitably arise in any relationship between individuals or organizations. However, relationships, output, and general well-being can all be strongly impacted by how disagreements are handled. This section examines the nature of conflict, the significance of conflict resolution, different conflict resolution techniques, and the abilities needed to effectively negotiate and settle disputes.

Diverse factors can give rise to conflicts, such as disparities in beliefs, principles, necessities, and passions. They can happen in communities, at work, in personal relationships, and even on a national and worldwide scale. Confrontations can take many different forms, including disagreements between people, problems inside organizations, and confrontations in the social or political spheres. Fundamentally, conflict arises when people or groups believe their behaviors or aims are incompatible. It's critical to understand that when handled properly, disagreement may really drive good development, inventiveness, and stronger bonds between people.

The power of conflict resolution to turn potentially harmful circumstances into chances for development and progress underscores its significance. A peaceful atmosphere may be fostered, tension can be decreased, and escalation can be avoided with effective conflict resolution. Constructive conflict resolution in interpersonal relationships can improve communication, deepen ties, and promote understanding. It can result in enhanced productivity, improved teamwork, and a healthy corporate culture at work. On a bigger scale, social cohesiveness, stability, and peace can result from resolving disputes inside communities and between nations.

Honest and open communication is one of the most critical tactics for successful conflict resolution. Effective communication is essential for comprehending and settling conflicts. It entails having a constructive conversation, carefully listening to the other person, and clearly expressing one's opinions and feelings. Active listening is essential because it shows respect and empathy, which helps the other person feel heard and appreciated. Conflicting parties can establish common ground and work toward a solution that is acceptable to both of them by understanding each other's needs and viewpoints.

Another crucial tactic in dispute resolution is negotiation. It entails a give-and-take procedure when parties talk about their disagreements and work to come to a decision that serves their respective interests. Finding win-win solutions is the primary goal of successful negotiation, along with flexibility and a willingness to compromise. It is crucial for negotiators to keep individuals apart from the issue, concentrate on shared interests rather than opposing viewpoints, and come up with solutions for both parties. Roger Fisher and William Ury popularized this strategy—known as principled negotiation—in their book "Getting to Yes." It highlights how crucial it is to resolve conflicts amicably while preserving relationships and working together to solve problems.

A neutral third person who guides the conversation and assists the disputing parties in reaching a conclusion is the mediator in a mediation. Instead of forcing a resolution, the mediator facilitates open dialogue and assists the parties in considering all of their choices. Mediation is beneficial for settling complicated or emotionally charged conflicts because it offers a controlled and encouraging setting for discussion. Mediators receive training on how to control the dynamics of disputes, deal with disparities in power, and advance a just and equitable settlement.

Arbitration is an additional method of resolving disputes; in this process, an impartial third party renders a legally binding judgment. In contrast to mediation, arbitration is a more formal process that resembles a court case. After both parties have presented their cases, the arbitrator makes a ruling. Arbitration is frequently utilized when a final resolution is required, such as in labor relations cases and commercial conflicts. Arbitration might not always address the underlying problems or foster the same degree of understanding as mediation, even though it offers a clear resolution.

Emotional intelligence, which includes the capacity to identify, comprehend, and regulate one's own emotions, as well as those of others, is another prerequisite for conflict resolution. People with emotional intelligence are better able to communicate clearly, handle conflict with poise, and show empathy for others. It helps people establish rapport, manage the emotional parts of conflict, and foster an atmosphere that is conducive to resolution. Self-awareness, self-regulation, social awareness, and relationship management abilities are all necessary for the development of emotional intelligence.

One of the most important aspects of conflict resolution is problem-solving. It entails determining the underlying reasons for the disagreement, coming up with potential fixes, and assessing the viability and significance of such fixes. To solve problems effectively, one needs to be creative, critical thinker, and cooperative. Conflicting parties can address their fundamental wants and interests by cooperating to develop solutions, as opposed to just treating the outward signs of their disagreement. This strategy may result in more enduring and fulfilling solutions.

Resolving conflicts also entails addressing power disparities and regulating power relations. Inequalities in power can impede successful communication and negotiation, making it challenging for weaker parties to stand out for their needs and interests. Establishing a secure and just atmosphere where everyone has an equal chance to engage and be heard is essential to addressing power disparities. This could call for the involvement of an impartial mediator, the application of particular communication strategies, or the establishment of rules and guidelines that support equity and inclusivity.

A crucial component of conflict resolution is cultural competence. Cultural differences can have a significant impact on how people view and handle problems. Recognizing the values, beliefs, and communication techniques of other ethnic groups is essential to appreciating and comprehending cultural diversity. In order to promote tolerance and respect for one another, conflict resolution techniques should be modified to account for cultural variations. This could entail becoming knowledgeable about cultural norms, avoiding ethnocentric presumptions, and maintaining an open mind to various viewpoints and methods.

Resolving conflicts in organizational contexts is crucial to preserving a supportive and effective work environment. Different tactics and procedures can be used by organizations to manage and avoid conflict. This entails developing precise guidelines and protocols for resolving disputes, offering educational opportunities, and cultivating an environment that values candid dialogue and teamwork. It is crucial for leaders to provide an example of good conflict resolution practices, resolve disputes quickly, and foster a supportive work environment. Organizations can improve worker engagement, satisfaction, and performance by encouraging a constructive conflict-resolution environment.

In community contexts, resolving conflicts entails including a variety of stakeholders and encouraging cooperative problem-solving. Social, economic, and environmental problems are only a few of the many possible causes of conflicts within a community. All parties impacted must be included in inclusive and participatory techniques for settlement to be adequate. Public consultations, community discussions, and cooperative decision-making procedures may all be part of this. Conflicts can be resolved in a way that represents the needs and interests of the whole community by incorporating individuals in the settlement process, which fosters social cohesion and resilience.

On a larger scale, diplomacy, negotiation, and peacebuilding initiatives are all part of national and international conflict resolution. The complexity and diversity of the issues involved in global conflicts necessitate the coordinated activities of many parties, including governments, international organizations, and civil society. In resolving international disputes, diplomacy and negotiation are essential because they seek to establish amicable and long-lasting solutions. The main objectives of peacebuilding initiatives are to deal with the underlying causes of conflict, encourage peacemaking, and assist in the establishment of structures and procedures that enable sustained peace and stability.

Conclusively, managing and resolving disputes in a constructive manner constitutes the multifarious and indispensable talent of conflict resolution. It covers a range of tactics, such as problem-solving, negotiation, mediation, arbitration, and open and honest communication. Cultural competency, emotional intelligence, and power dynamics management are necessary for effective conflict resolution. Conflict resolution is essential for fostering mutual understanding, teamwork, and successful outcomes in interpersonal interactions as well as in the business, community, and national and international arenas. Individuals and organizations can turn problems into chances for development, creativity, and better relationships by learning and using conflict resolution techniques, which will ultimately lead to a more peaceful and effective society.

CHAPTER VI

Enhancing Productivity and Efficiency

Time Management

Effective time management is a crucial ability that affects stress levels, output, and general quality of life. To effectively accomplish goals, it includes organizing, prioritizing, scheduling, and managing the amount of time spent on various tasks. Making the most of one's time through effective time management helps people achieve better results on a personal and professional level. This section discusses the value of time management, several ways to improve it, typical problems, and the advantages of becoming proficient in this crucial ability.

In today's fast-paced world of constant demands and distractions, time management is essential. It enables people to complete more tasks in less time, which may increase output and success. Effective time management allows people to set aside enough time for critical tasks, cut down on procrastination, and reliably fulfill deadlines. This improves output and establishes a reputation for dependability and effectiveness. Furthermore, effective time management lessens stress since it gives one a sense of control and lessens the chaos that frequently results from inadequate planning.

Having specific goals is one of the core components of time management. Setting goals gives people a sense of purpose and direction for what is to be done. Setting SMART (specific, measurable, attainable, relevant, and time-bound) goals is a necessary step in practical goal setting. It is simpler to allocate time and resources efficiently when there is a framework in place to guarantee that goals are achievable within a given time frame. An example of a SMART goal would be to "exercise for 30 minutes, five days a week, for the next three months," as opposed to aiming for something more general like "improve fitness."

Another essential element of time management is planning. Planning is laying out a schedule for achieving objectives by dividing them into more manageable, more minor activities. An organized strategy makes it easier for people to stay focused and organized while making sure they allot their time wisely to each assignment. Digital apps, planners, and calendars are examples of tools that might help in this procedure. People can better manage their time and stay on task by, for instance, scheduling tasks and setting reminders with a digital calendar.

Setting priorities is crucial to efficient time management. Setting priorities enables people to concentrate on the things that really matter because not all tasks are created equal. A well-liked method for prioritizing tasks, the Eisenhower Matrix divides them into four quadrants according to their significance and urgency. Using this technique, people may determine which chores need to be completed right away, which ones can wait until later, which ones can be assigned, and which ones can be dropped. People may make sure they are spending their time and energy on things that are most impactful and in line with their goals by setting priorities for their tasks.

The Pomodoro Technique is another essential time management technique. Using this strategy, work is divided into intervals, usually lasting 25 minutes each, and then a brief rest is taken. This strategy lessens burnout while preserving productivity and focus. People can rejuvenate during regular breaks, which lessens weariness and helps them perform at a high level all day. In addition to instilling a sense of urgency, the Pomodoro Technique motivates people to finish activities within the allotted time.

A key component of time management, particularly in work environments, is delegation. Task delegation empowers team members and promotes teamwork in addition to freeing up time for more crucial activities. Delegating effectively entails determining whether activities are capable of being completed by others, outlining expectations in detail, and supplying the required tools and assistance. People who delegate authority to others are able to concentrate on high-priority tasks that demand their knowledge and attention
.

Resolving procrastination is essential to time management success. The propensity to put off things until the last minute usually results in tension and last-minute rushes. People can deal with procrastination by being aware of its root reasons, which might include perfectionism, fear of failing, or a lack of drive. Procrastination can be avoided by adopting techniques like breaking things down into manageable chunks, setting deadlines, removing distractions, and rewarding oneself when chores are finished. Additionally effective at reducing procrastination are the cultivation of self-discipline and the creation of a favorable work environment.

Effective distraction control is another aspect of time management. Distractions are commonplace in the digital era of today, ranging from continuous email alerts to social media updates. Retaining focus and productivity requires recognizing and reducing distractions. Turning off notifications, utilizing internet blockers, and designating a specific workspace are a few strategies that can assist people in maintaining task focus. You can also avoid work interruptions from social media and email checks by scheduling distinct hours for these activities.

One of the most crucial aspects of time management is work-life balance. Establishing a schedule that accommodates work and leisure activities helps people stay healthy overall. Burnout brought on by overworking can have a detrimental effect on one's productivity and health. Setting limits and scheduling downtime for hobbies, leisure, and quality time with loved ones is crucial. People can recharge thanks to this balance, which lowers stress and raises happiness levels all around.

Another aspect of efficient time management is routinely reflecting on and assessing one's progress. People who reflect on a regular basis are better able to evaluate their time management skills and pinpoint opportunities for development. Maintaining a time log or journal can reveal patterns of productivity and procrastination and offer insights into how time is spent. Individuals can modify their plans, make new objectives, and keep honing their time management techniques with the help of regular reviews.

Overcoming unforeseen circumstances and disruptions is one of the difficulties in time management. Adaptability and flexibility are critical traits in handling these kinds of circumstances. Setting priorities and making goals is vital, but it's also crucial to be flexible and modify plans in the event that unanticipated events occur. Even in situations where plans do not work out, people can still efficiently manage their time by creating backup plans and learning how to reorder their priorities.

The propensity to overcommit presents another difficulty with time management. Assuming an excessive amount of obligations might cause stress and lower productivity. It's critical to develop the ability to say no and to set reasonable deadlines for tasks that must be completed. It is possible to avoid overcommitting and make sure that time is spent on worthwhile activities by assessing commitments and concentrating on tasks that support both personal and professional goals.

Individual differences in work styles, interests, and personalities also have an impact on time management.

Comprehending one's innate cycles and inclinations might facilitate the customization of time management tactics to meet personal requirements. For instance, some people work best in the afternoon or evening, while others could be more productive in the morning. It is possible to increase productivity and effectiveness by identifying these trends and allocating duties appropriately.

Time management is significantly impacted by technology. There are numerous apps and tools available to help with time management, scheduling, and planning. People may stay organized and efficiently manage their time with the use of tools like productivity applications, time-tracking software, and project management software. But it's crucial to utilize technology sensibly and keep from getting overwhelmed by the abundance of choices. Selecting tools that suit individual requirements and tastes helps improve time management without needlessly complicating things.

Time management techniques have several advantages. One of the most significant advantages is increased productivity since people can do more tasks in less time. Motivation and morale are raised as a result of feeling satisfied and accomplished. Good time management also eases the strain of last-minute rushes and gives one a sense of control, both of which lower stress levels. People can preserve their general well-being and avoid burnout by making time for self-care and relaxation.

Successful time management in the workplace can advance one's career. It makes it possible for people to regularly fulfill deadlines, generate excellent work, and seize new chances. Recognition, job promotions, and professional development may result from this. Furthermore, businesses place great value on effective time management since it fosters a happy work atmosphere and overall organizational performance.

In the personal sphere, efficient time management enables people to follow their hobbies, spend time with those they love, and maintain a positive work-life balance. It makes it possible for people to set aside time for pursuits that make them happy and fulfilled, improving their general quality of life. Effective time management enables people to seek personal development, which results in a more contented and significant existence.

In academic environments, time management is also critical. For students, juggling extracurricular activities, personal obligations, and coursework requires good time management. Early on in life, acquiring practical time management skills can provide the groundwork for success later on. Students can effectively manage their workload and attain academic achievement by implementing strategies, including making study plans, establishing goals, and assigning priorities.

To sum up, time management is an essential ability that affects stress levels, output, and general quality of life. It entails planning, prioritizing, defining specific objectives, and efficiently handling distractions. Flexibility, self-control, and adaptability are necessary to overcome obstacles, including procrastination, overcommitment, and unforeseen disruptions. Good time management has several advantages, such as increased job success, decreased stress, increased productivity, and a better work-life balance. People can make the most of their time, accomplish their goals, and lead more purposeful and meaningful lives by becoming adept at time management.

Workplace Organization

Organization in the workplace is crucial to any company's production and effectiveness. It includes a range of tactics and procedures intended to guarantee the efficient and successful operation of an organization. A well-organized workplace encompasses various aspects, such as the arrangement of the workspace, efficient workflow management, and the cultivation of a healthy company culture. The goal is to establish a work environment that minimizes obstacles to employees' task performance, hence optimizing their productivity and job happiness.'

The physical layout of the workstation is one of the fundamental components of workplace organization. This entails allocating desks, tools, and resources strategically in order to maximize productivity and communication. The physical arrangement should take into account things like noise levels, natural light, and the distance to colleagues and essential instruments. For example, an open-plan workplace might let team members communicate and work together more effectively. For activities that need seclusion and concentration, cubicles or private offices might be a preferable option. Additionally, ergonomic factors are essential because they can reduce workplace accidents and promote comfort, both of which boost productivity.

The administration of digital resources is a crucial component of workplace structure. Digital organization is equally as important as physical organization in today's technologically advanced environment. To make information easily accessible and well-organized, this involves arranging electronic files, communications, and software systems. Efficiency is increased when information and documents are found more quickly through effective digital organization. Better organization and cooperation can also be facilitated by putting project management software and cloud storage solutions into place, especially for remote teams.

One further essential component of workplace organization is efficient workflow management. This entails creating procedures that minimize pointless steps and streamline work. In order to find bottlenecks and potential improvement areas, workflow management frequently necessitates a thorough investigation of the current processes. Process optimization and waste reduction can be achieved by utilizing methodologies like Six Sigma and Lean management. Organizations may guarantee that work is done more quickly, that deadlines are met, and that resources are used wisely by streamlining workflows.

Organization in the workplace also includes time and priority management. Employees can better manage their workloads by using time management techniques like the Pomodoro Technique, time blocking, and prioritization frameworks like the Eisenhower Matrix. Encouraging employees to utilize these tactics can help them approach their work in a more organized and controllable way, which can reduce stress and prevent burnout. Regular time management training and seminars can also help to provide staff members with the skills they need to efficiently plan their workload.

One cannot stress the importance of leadership in creating a well-organized workplace. Leaders set the standard for the entire company, and their staff members frequently share their dedication to efficiency and order. In addition to endorsing organizational procedures, competent leaders ought to provide an example for these actions. This entails keeping one's workspace tidy and orderly, arriving on time, and following rules and procedures. In addition, managers ought to promote candid dialogue and feedback so that staff members can express their ideas and worries about how the workplace is run.

An essential element of workplace organization is communication. Ensuring that all team members understand their duties and responsibilities and are in agreement is ensured by clear and consistent communication. Whether they are monthly evaluations, weekly check-ins, or daily stand-ups, regular meetings can keep everyone informed and in sync. Better coordination can be facilitated by using communication technologies like Slack, Microsoft Teams, or Zoom, particularly for distributed or remote teams. Active listening is another component of effective communication, where managers and team members are urged to actively listen to each other's suggestions and opinions.

An essential component of workplace organization is the development of a positive organizational culture. Collaboration, creativity, and job satisfaction are all enhanced by a positive workplace culture and lead to a more orderly and efficient work environment. This entails establishing a setting where workers are inspired and feel appreciated. Within the company, initiatives like team-building exercises, recognition programs, and professional development opportunities can boost morale and create a feeling of community. Positive workplace cultures also inspire staff members to take charge of their workflows and workplaces, which improves efficiency and organization.

The structure of the workplace must take health and safety into account in addition to these other factors. An office that puts its workers' health and safety first is well-organized. This entails making sure that there are no risks in the workspace, that emergency processes are in place, and that staff members have received health and safety training. Potential safety hazards can be found and fixed with the assistance of routine maintenance and inspections before they become issues. A healthier and more effective workforce can also result from supporting wellness efforts, including exercise programs, mental health counseling, and ergonomic assessments.

Technology integration is yet another essential component of workplace structure. Technology may increase productivity, facilitate collaboration, and expedite procedures. Automation systems, for instance, can manage monotonous jobs, freeing up staff members to concentrate on more intricate and strategic work. Organizations can improve the efficiency of their operations by implementing enterprise resource planning (ERP) software, customer relationship management (CRM) systems, and other technology solutions. However, it's crucial to make sure staff members have the necessary training to utilize these tools efficiently and that technical assistance is offered for any problems that may come up.

In the workplace, development, and training are essential components. Employees who engage in continuous learning are guaranteed to possess the newest abilities and know-how necessary to carry out their jobs effectively. Providing staff with access to online courses, workshops, and regular training sessions can help them keep current on industry trends and best practices. Furthermore, when employees feel appreciated and perceive room for advancement within the company, investing in their professional development can result in increased job satisfaction and retention rates.

An increasingly important factor in workplace organization is sustainability. Incorporating sustainable practices into workplace organizations can improve the environment, and the company's reputation as organizations become more conscious of their environmental impact. This can involve taking steps like utilizing energy-efficient equipment, instituting recycling programs, and cutting back on paper use. Businesses that embrace sustainability can draw in eco-aware customers and staff in addition to aiding in environmental preservation.

The importance of flexibility in today's working structures is growing. The conventional 9–5 workday is changing as more companies provide flexible work schedules like flextime, remote work, and shortened work weeks. Reduced commute times, a better work-life balance, and higher job satisfaction can all be achieved with flexible work arrangements. However, to preserve productivity and communication, managing a flexible workforce calls for meticulous planning and structure. The intricacies of a flexible work environment can be handled with the aid of digital collaboration tools and the establishment of explicit standards and expectations.

Another crucial component of workplace organization is change management. In the current dynamic business landscape, enterprises need to possess the agility and the capacity to adjust promptly to changes. Achieving effective change management entails assisting, encouraging, and guiding staff members as they adjust to changes. This entails giving concise explanations of the change's motivations, offering assistance with any questions or difficulties that may come up, and supplying tools and training to ease the transition. Employee adoption of new working practices can be facilitated and disruptions reduced by a well-run change management procedure.

Inclusion and diversity are crucial elements of workplace structure as well. People with various viewpoints, experiences, and backgrounds come together in a diverse and inclusive workplace, which fosters innovation and enhances decision-making. Fostering an atmosphere where each employee feels appreciated and respected is essential to promoting diversity and inclusion. This can involve putting anti-discrimination policies into place, offering diversity education, and fostering an inclusive culture. Organizations may build a more dynamic and productive workplace by fostering diversity and inclusion.

Human resources (HR) plays a variety of roles in workplace organizations. Hiring, onboarding, and employee retention are all under HR's purview and are necessary to keep a productive and well-organized workplace. In addition, HR is crucial to the creation and execution of policies and procedures that support workplace organization, including employee handbooks, performance management systems, and health and safety guidelines. HR can also help managers and staff members overcome organizational obstacles and enhance workplace organization by offering resources and support.

The idea of continuous improvement ought to guide every facet of workplace structure. To find opportunities for improvement, organizations should routinely assess their procedures, practices, and policies. This may entail conducting audits, getting input from staff members, and comparing results to industry norms. Through the adoption of a continuous improvement mindset, organizations can maintain a competitive edge and consistently improve their productivity and efficiency.

To sum up, workplace organization encompasses a variety of elements, including the thoughtful placement of both digital and physical resources, efficient workflow and time management, strong leadership, transparent communication, and the development of a positive company culture. It also covers issues related to health and safety, technology integration, ongoing education and training, flexibility, change management, diversity and inclusion, and the function of human resources. Organizations can foster an environment where workers can carry out their responsibilities effectively and efficiently by addressing these different factors, which will boost output, job satisfaction, and overall success.

Continuous Learning and Development

The ideas of continuous learning and development are closely linked to the growth and development of people, groups, and society at large. The significance of these ideas cannot be emphasized in a time of swift technological progress, global interconnectedness, and a constantly changing labor market. The process of continuously learning new skills, competencies, and knowledge throughout one's life is referred to as continuous learning and development. This process, which promotes flexibility, ingenuity, and resilience in the face of change, is essential for one's own development, professional progression, and the advancement of society as a whole.

The rate of technical advancement in the present world is unheard of. While specific skills become outdated, innovations in biotechnology, machine learning, artificial intelligence, and other sectors are changing industries and opening up new opportunities. A vital skill in such a changing environment is the capacity for ongoing learning. People have to learn how to adjust to new technology and methods in addition to keeping up with the most recent developments. Beyond merely mastering technical skills, this ongoing education includes critical thinking, problem-solving, and flexibility. People who embrace lifelong learning are better equipped to handle the challenges of the contemporary world, stay relevant in their line of work, and make significant contributions to society.

One crucial setting where ongoing learning and development take happen is the workplace. The ability to learn and adapt is valued in the modern workplace just as much as or even more than prior expertise. Companies understand that encouraging a culture of lifelong learning may boost creativity, output, and worker happiness. Businesses that support the professional growth of their staff are more likely to hold onto top personnel and keep a competitive advantage. This investment can come in a number of forms, such as access to online learning resources, mentorship, and official training programs. Organizations that encourage continuous learning help to develop a more engaged and motivated workforce in addition to improving the capabilities of their personnel.

Ongoing education and development are closely related to personal growth and fulfillment. A stronger sense of purpose and contentment in life might result from pursuing knowledge and self-improvement. People are encouraged to confront their preconceptions, broaden their views, and seek new interests through continuous learning. It promotes a growth mentality, which is defined as the conviction that one can achieve improvement and growth with hard work and persistence. This kind of thinking makes people more resilient to setbacks and more eager to try new, challenging things. People who are growing and changing have higher levels of confidence and self-efficacy, which has a beneficial effect on every aspect of their lives.

Early instillation of the values of lifelong learning and development is greatly aided by the school system. There is a growing trend in education to complement traditional models, which concentrate on rote memorization and standardized testing, with methods that place more emphasis on critical thinking, creativity, and problem-solving abilities. Teachers are realizing that teaching kids how to learn is just as important as teaching them what to know. Schools create a desire and passion for learning in their students, preparing them to be lifelong learners. As people go into higher education and the workforce, where they must constantly update their knowledge and skills to thrive, this foundation is crucial.

The introduction of digital technology has dramatically increased accessibility to professional and educational opportunities for all. There are a plethora of courses available on almost any topic through online learning platforms like Coursera, edX, and LinkedIn Learning. With the freedom to study at their own speed and in their own timeframe that these tools offer, juggling work and personal obligations is made simpler. Additionally, people can seek specialized information and skills through online learning that might not be easily accessible through regular educational institutions. Regardless of their location or circumstances, anyone can engage in ongoing learning and development by utilizing these tools.

In today's world, career advancement greatly depends on ongoing education and training. Today's professionals are likely to undergo many job changes over their working lifetimes, in contrast to past generations who may have worked for a single company throughout their careers. Every transfer could call for learning new abilities and information. People who make a commitment to lifelong learning are better able to handle these changes and take advantage of new opportunities as they present themselves. Furthermore, the skill to pick things up fast and adapt makes a person more appealing to employers because it shows that they can survive in a dynamic setting.

Another crucial area where constant learning is essential is leadership development. A wide range of abilities, such as communication, emotional intelligence, and strategic thinking, are necessary for effective leadership. These abilities need to be continuously developed in order to meet new difficulties and situations. They are not static. Continuously learning leaders are better able to motivate and steer their teams, propel the success of their organizations, and handle the complexities of today's business climate. Peer learning networks, executive coaching, and leadership development programs are just a few of the ways that leaders can continue to grow.

Ongoing education and growth are also significant drivers of society's advancement. It is more crucial than ever to be able to comprehend and value other points of view in our increasingly international society. Ongoing education promotes curiosity about other people's cultures, history, and worldviews, which increases empathy and teamwork. Addressing complicated global issues like social injustice, public health, and climate change requires this kind of cultural competency. Societies can develop more informed and involved citizens who can work for the common good by encouraging lifelong learning.

Continuous learning and development are also essential for maintaining one's own health and well-being. New discoveries in healthcare and medical research bring us fresh perspectives on how to have longer, better lives. People can improve their physical, mental, and emotional well-being by learning about these advancements and implementing good behaviors into their daily lives. In this context, continuous learning entails being proactive with one's health, searching out trustworthy information, and remaining open to new ideas. A higher quality of life and improved health are the results of this proactive approach.

The humanities and arts are essential to lifelong learning and growth. In addition to promoting intellectual and emotional development, exposure to literature, music, visual arts, and other cultural manifestations offers profound insights into the human condition. A well-rounded education must include contemplation, self-expression, and creativity, all of which are enhanced by the arts. Through engaging with the arts, people can cultivate a lifetime of respect for intellectual and cultural endeavors as well as a deeper understanding of themselves and the world around them.

Even while lifelong learning and growth have numerous advantages, there are always issues that need to be resolved. The risk of information overload is one of the main challenges. It might be challenging to determine what is trustworthy and relevant in an era when information is widely available. Gaining information literacy and critical thinking abilities is crucial for surviving in this environment. People need to develop their ability to assess sources, recognize biases, and combine data from various viewpoints. Making educated decisions and avoiding the traps of false information require this discernment.

Fair access to educational opportunities is yet another critical issue. Even though more people can now attend education, thanks to online learning platforms, there are still gaps in educational opportunities depending on things like socioeconomic level, region, and technology access. The public and commercial sectors must work together to address these gaps in education and healthcare. To make sure that everyone has the opportunity to engage in ongoing learning and development, policies and programs that support digital inclusion, reasonably priced education, and opportunities for lifetime learning are crucial.

Time management and motivation are essential for everyone who wants to pursue lifelong learning. It might be challenging to juggle education with obligations to your family, job, and social life. People can incorporate learning into their daily lives by creating realistic goals and using efficient time management techniques. Furthermore, extrinsic motivation—which is dependent on outside demands or rewards—is frequently less lasting than intrinsic motivation, which is fueled by a sincere interest and love of learning. Developing a passion for education and a feeling of purpose might help people persevere through the inevitable obstacles and disappointments they may experience while pursuing their educational goals.

In the framework of ongoing learning and growth, peer mentoring and learning play a crucial role. Through mentoring, people can get advice, support, and insightful knowledge from more seasoned experts. Effective career navigation can be facilitated by a solid mentor-mentee relationship, which helps quicken learning and development. In a similar vein, peer learning promotes a cooperative atmosphere where people may discuss ideas, share knowledge, and benefit from one another's experiences. This collaborative approach to education fosters creativity, improves problem-solving skills, and strengthens a sense of community.

Success in an organization also depends on ongoing learning and development. For enterprises to prosper in a business climate that is changing quickly, they need to be flexible and agile. Organizations may remain ahead of industry trends, efficiently address market demands, and stimulate innovation by cultivating a culture of continuous learning. This culture is developed by the dedication of the leadership, the funding of staff training, and the establishment of a risk-taking and experimental atmosphere. Businesses that place a high priority on ongoing learning will be more sustainable and prosperous in the long run.

Informal learning experiences are included in the concept of continuous learning, which goes beyond formal schooling and professional growth. Informal learning happens through regular activities, including reading, interacting with others, and getting hands-on experience. It is frequently self-directed and motivated by a person's curiosity and interests. By offering knowledge and skills in real-world applications, informal learning enhances formal education. Fostering a comprehensive approach to ongoing learning and growth requires acknowledging and appreciating informal learning experiences.

Apart from personal endeavors, social frameworks, and regulations are crucial in fostering ongoing education and growth. To foster an environment that supports lifelong learning, corporations, governments, and educational institutions must work together. This includes establishing infrastructure that supports learning, sponsoring training and development initiatives, and formulating regulations that support educational access. Infrastructures such as community centers, public libraries, and internet resources can facilitate lifelong learning. Societies may invest in these resources to produce a population that is better educated and competent, equipped to tackle social issues and propel economic progress.

There are benefits and drawbacks to the convergence of technology and ongoing education. On the one hand, technology has completely changed how people can access knowledge and education, allowing them to learn at any time or place. Virtual classrooms, webinars, and online courses have increased accessibility and flexibility in education. On the other hand, keeping up with new advancements might be difficult due to the quick speed of technological progress. In this environment, continuous learning necessitates that people keep up with technological developments and acquire the abilities necessary to effectively use new tools and platforms.

There is growing recognition of the need for lifelong learning in tackling societal issues.

Creative solutions and an informed public are needed for complex global concerns like public health, economic injustice, and climate change. Individuals who engage in continuous learning acquire the information and abilities required to comprehend and tackle these difficulties. It encourages teamwork, creativity, and critical thinking—all skills necessary for coming up with workable solutions. Societies can improve their ability to address urgent problems and create a more just and sustainable future by encouraging lifelong learning.

Continuous learning and development are essential for promoting innovation and competitiveness in the context of economic growth. The capacity to create new concepts, innovate technology, and enhance existing procedures is necessary for economic expansion in a knowledge-based economy. Maintaining a competitive edge, fostering innovation, and staying at the forefront of one's sector are all made possible by continuous learning for both individuals and businesses. Governments and corporations that allocate resources towards education and training stand to gain an advantage in developing highly-trained labor pools, drawing in the capital, and promoting economic growth.

In the context of aging populations, the idea of ongoing learning and development is equally pertinent. The need for continued learning and skill development increases as people live longer, healthier lives. Seniors' quality of life can be improved by lifelong learning because it offers chances for personal fulfillment, social contact, and intellectual engagement. Additionally, utilizing their experience and skills to benefit the community can assist senior citizens in continuing to be engaged and productive members of society. Communities can become more dynamic and inclusive when societies encourage lifelong learning for all age groups.

A mental shift is needed to incorporate constant learning into daily living. It entails realizing that learning is a continuous process that is not limited to formal education or particular life periods. People must embrace this change by taking charge of their education, looking for chances to improve, and keeping an open mind to new things. In order to support this mindset, businesses, and educational institutions must also establish settings that promote experimentation, discovery, and ongoing development.

To sum up, lifelong learning and growth are necessary for adjusting to the challenges of the contemporary world, developing professionally and personally, and advancing society. The necessity for people and businesses to embrace lifelong learning is highlighted by the quick speed of technological change, the changing nature of employment, and the growing complexity of global concerns. People who make a commitment to lifelong learning can improve their abilities, seize new chances, and have happy, whole lives. Companies can retain top personnel, stimulate innovation, and stay competitive by cultivating a culture of learning. Communities that value lifelong learning can become better informed, resilient, and involved, enabling them to tackle urgent issues and create sustainable futures.

There are difficulties along the path of lifelong learning and growth. Time management, motivation, fair access, and information overload are significant challenges that need to be overcome. Nevertheless, these difficulties are surmountable if the appropriate plans and resources are put in place. Through cultivating a passion for learning, advancing digital inclusiveness, and strengthening critical thinking abilities, people and societies can overcome these challenges and fully reap the rewards of lifelong learning.

Ultimately, gaining new knowledge and abilities isn't the only goal of constant learning and development. They focus on developing an attitude of inquiry, flexibility, and continuous improvement. In an environment where novelty is the only thing that remains constant, the capacity for lifelong learning and evolution is not just an advantageous trait but also a necessary survival skill. Unlocking our full potential and navigating the intricacies of the modern world depend on ongoing learning and development, whether in the context of societal progress, professional success, or personal growth. We can build a more promising, inventive, and inclusive future for everybody by embracing this path. The future belongs to those who are willing to continuously learn, grow, and adapt.

CONCLUSION

It is evident by the book's conclusion, "The Kaizen Way: Embracing Small Changes for Big Impact," that the Kaizen philosophy offers a potent and revolutionary strategy for both professional and personal development. We may make significant, long-lasting changes without taking overwhelming, extreme measures if we adopt the concepts of continuous development. The secret to success is the determination to steadily make tiny, gradual advancements over time.

We have examined the history and fundamental ideas of Kaizen throughout this book, showing how this Japanese way of thinking has impacted some of the most prosperous businesses in the world. From its inception in Japan following World War II to its broad implementation in international company operations, Kaizen has shown itself to be a flexible and successful tactic for promoting advancement and creativity. Kaizen promotes a continuous improvement culture that may be used in both personal and professional contexts by emphasizing group development rather than drastic change.

Kaizen urges us to find areas in our daily lives where we can improve and make modest, doable adjustments that add up to significant outcomes over time. The simplicity and sustainability of Kaizen reside in its potential to help us improve our abilities, relationships, and behaviors while also being simple and sustainable. We can gain momentum and accomplish our long-term objectives by beginning modestly and continuing to be consistent.

Think about the customs and practices that you follow on a daily basis. You can establish a positive feedback loop that leads to significant increases in your well-being by adopting small changes, like walking for short periods of time every day, progressively altering your nutrition, or setting aside a few minutes each day to practice mindfulness. Even if these modest deeds don't seem like much on their own, over time, they can have a cumulative effect that completely changes your life.

Within the context of the workplace, Kaizen provides a structure for improving output, effectiveness, and creativity. Companies can empower staff members to contribute to the success of the company at all levels by cultivating a culture of continuous improvement. This enhances operational performance and fosters a productive workplace where innovation and teamwork are encouraged.

Promoting input and improvement recommendations from all team members is a crucial component of implementing Kaizen in the workplace. The performance of an organization can be significantly impacted by actions like encouraging experimentation, holding frequent feedback sessions, and recognizing modest victories. Businesses may create strong teams, generate strong leadership, and promote sustainable growth by implementing Kaizen concepts.

This book's examples of successful implementations in real-world settings attest to the transformational potential of Kaizen. These case studies demonstrate how Kaizen's ideas are applicable everywhere and are derived from both personal and business experiences. These stories, which range from people who have improved their health and wellbeing by tiny, regular adjustments for companies that have improved their operations and seen incredible success, demonstrate the potential of Kaizen to have a significant and long-lasting influence.

Recalling the lessons and tactics discussed in "The Kaizen Way: Embracing Small Changes for Big Impact," it's critical to keep in mind that the pursuit of continuous improvement is a constant process. Kaizen's genuine essence is found in its dedication to continuous improvement and growth. You may continue to apply Kaizen ideas to every aspect of your life by keeping an open mind and being willing to take small steps forward.

Kaizen is a lifelong pursuit of tiny, intentional activities rather than a rapid fix. You will accomplish your goals and have a more tremendous respect for the process of constant growth if you take this mentality. These minor adjustments will have a massive impact on many facets of your life and provide the groundwork for long-term success and happiness, far beyond the apparent effects.

To sum up, "The Kaizen Way: Embracing Small Changes for Big Impact" is a valuable and motivational manual for appreciating the significance of gradual, tiny advancements. Applying the concepts of Kaizen to one's professional or personal development offers a viable way to bring about meaningful and long-lasting change. You can realize your full potential and design a life of constant advancement and success by adhering to this idea.